ACKNOWLEDGEMENTS

The authors and publishers gratefully acknowledge the following sources which made available the data incorporated in many of the maps throughout this book.
The Changing Face of Toronto, Donald Kerr and Jacob Spelt, Geographical Branch, Department of Mines and Technical Surveys, Queen's Printer, Ottawa / 27, 40, 50
City of Toronto / 121
Mrs. Earl C. Shaw / 28
Economic Atlas of Ontario/Atlas Economique de l'Ontario by W. G. Dean (Editor) and G. J. Matthews (Cartographer). University of Toronto Press for the Government of Ontario / 17, 56, 57, 68 (bottom), 109, 113 (right), 114 (both), 115 (both)
Government of Ontario / 16 (top left), 32, 80 (all), 81 (all), 84 (both), 85 (both), 112, 116
Metro Roads and Traffic Department / 13 (bottom left), 102
Metropolitan Toronto Planning Board / 3, 11, 35, 66 (left), 71, 81 (bottom), 82, 86, 87, 90 (both), 91 (both), 100 (both), 101, 102 (left), 122, 124, 125 , envelope
Metropolitan Toronto Public Library / 20 (right), 22
Metropolitan Toronto Social Planning Council / 107, 70
Ontario Department of Energy and Resources Management / 110, 111
Ontario Department of Trade and Commerce / 126
Ontario Hydro / 89
From Regional and Resource Planning in Canada, edited by Ralph R. Kreuger, Frederic O. Sargent, Anthony de Vos, Norman Pearson. Copyright © 1963 by Holt, Rinehart and Winston of Canada Limited. Reprinted by permission of Holt, Rinehart and Winston of Canada Limited, Publishers, Toronto. / 113
Toronto During the French Régime 1615-1793, Percy J. Robinson. University of Toronto Press / 20
Toronto Real Estate Board / 78

The authors and publishers also wish to thank the following organizations which made available the photographs on the pages listed.
Canada Steamship Lines, Montreal / 21
Central Mortgage and Housing Corporation / 74 (right), 75 (C, D, E, F, G)
Department of Mines, Energy and Resources, Ottawa / 39, 44 (left), 50, 54, 55 (left), 73 (left), 75 (right), 87 (left), 88, 92 (top), 96
Lockwood Survey Corporation Limited, Toronto /envelope, 7, 14 (top right), 15 (bottom), 35 (both), 43, 44 (right), 46, 55 (right), 74 (left), 86 (left), 92 (bottom), 104 (bottom right), 123 (top)
Ontario Department of Tourism and Information / 6, 8 (bottom), 9 (top left), 14 (top left), 42, 45, 76 (B), 104 (top left, top two right, left and right middle, bottom left)
Ontario Hydro / 9 (top right, bottom)
Parkin Architects, Engineers, Planners, 1500 Don Mills Rd., Don Mills 404, Toronto, Canada / 75 (left), 123 (bottom)
Paul Shakespeare / 2, 8 (top), 10, 14 (bottom two), 15 (top two), 37 (both), 49 (all), 58 (left), 73 (right), 76 (A), 86 (right), 95 (all) 104 (second left, middle, bottom middle)
Roger Jowett, Photographer, Willowdale / 57
Ron Vickers Ltd., Photography, Toronto 105
Royal Ontario Museum, Toronto / 23 (both), 25
Toronto Public Library, John Ross Robertson Collection / 29, 30
University of Toronto / 32

Maps and Graphs by Antony Bradshaw and Charles Goode

URBAN STUDIES SERIES

General Editor:

RICHARD P. BAINE

Series Consultant:

JOHN W. WARKENTIN
Chairman
Department of Geography
York University, Toronto

TORONTO AN URBAN STUDY

RICHARD P. BAINE
Associate Professor of Geography
The College of Education
University of Toronto

A. LYNN McMURRAY
Head of the Geography Department
North Toronto Collegiate Institute
City of Toronto

CLARKE, IRWIN & COMPANY LIMITED / TORONTO, VANCOUVER

W9-ABK-342

LIST OF MAPS, CHARTS, GRAPHS AND DIAGRAMS

LIST OF STATISTICAL TABLES

© 1970 by Clarke, Irwin & Company Limited

ISBN 0 7720 0483 8

Printed in Canada

1 2 3 4 5 AP 74 73 72 71 70

INTRODUCTION

We live in an urban age. Almost three quarters of the Canadian populace reside and work in towns and cities. And the proportion is rapidly rising. It is therefore of crucial importance that we gain at least a general knowledge of what a city is—what causes it to form and develop, what elements go together to make it up, and how these elements act upon each other to create our often overwhelming and bewildering urban environments. Without such knowledge, we will be ill-prepared to improve the quality of urban life. This book, accordingly, has been designed to do two things: first, to reveal to the reader the landscape of Toronto—an excellent example of a major multifunctional metropolis; second, to introduce him, through the example of Toronto, to some of the fundamental concepts and procedures of urban geography.

The format of TORONTO is a major departure from that of the standard textbook. It is essentially a compilation of carefully selected materials in the form of photographs, maps, charts, diagrams, and statistics. There is little expository writing. Each item has something significant to say about Toronto in particular and about big cities in general. Some items, of course, can be analyzed to a far greater degree than others, but every one warrants more than cursory attention. The reader is presented with the evidence of *what is there* in Toronto and is given the opportunity to observe and analyze and thus to discover for himself something of what a big city is.

So that the book may be used for a variety of purposes and in a variety of ways, we have avoided a rigid organization. The various sections have been designed and arranged in such a way as to provide the reader with the opportunity to freely and imaginatively select materials and to follow any order he may feel appropriate to his needs. To study a particular topic or theme, such as the implications of building the Spadina Expressway for example, one might start by examining a particular photograph in one part of the book, refer to a table in another part, and then examine a map in yet another part. Those who wish to proceed through the book from beginning to end, nevertheless, will find the sequence logical and the learning cumulative.

There are distinct advantages in studying data that are set out in a variety of forms. For one thing, a feature or a concept is presented from not just one but several points of view, and the more ways one looks at something the more clearly he sees it. The characteristics of Toronto's Central Business District, for example, are revealed in photographs taken from various angles, on maps, in statistical tables, in graphs, and in written descriptions. For another thing, several kinds of thinking are brought into play in working with so many different materials. Maps are to be interpreted, statistics translated into graphs, calculations made, photographs analyzed, value judgements rendered, and plans developed. Finally, the reader is made aware of the many sources of information available to him should he wish to pursue further the studies that have been introduced in this book.

The organization of each section is quite simple. First, the subject is introduced in a brief exposition that deals with its basic nature and significance and gives a general idea of what follows. Next, there is a set of *focal points*. These are guidelines that suggest to the reader some ideas he might concentrate on and the analytical procedures he might adopt as he examines the materials. Suggestions are not spelled out in detail, because, as far as possible, the materials are to *speak for themselves,* to be used as evidence that can lead to important and worthwhile discoveries. Implicit throughout, of course, are the questions *Why?* and *How?* Following the focal points are the materials themselves. Some of the more unusual items have explanatory statements accompanying them; most of the items, however, stand on their own. The map Existing Land Use, 1968, for the Metropolitan Toronto Planning Area and an air mosaic that shows the full extent of Metropolitan Toronto for the year 1969 are to be found in the envelope at the back of the book. They have been kept separate because they are likely to be used more frequently than anything else. An enormous amount of information is compressed into these two items. All the general land use patterns of the city, the basic arrangement of its parts, its shape and extent, the broad features of its site, the lines of thrust of its development, and many of its basic problems are there to be observed and reflected upon. Further, both of these items can be employed to provide the general geographical context for more particular studies. The Street Map of Metropolitan Toronto (1-3) on page 3 will also prove valuable for general reference purposes.

Several major area divisions are used in this book. *Toronto* refers to the whole urban complex that contains and spills over the limits of the corporation known as Metropolitan Toronto. It is a general term, in other words, that applies to an area for which it is impossible to draw a hard and fast boundary. *Metropolitan Toronto* is a municipality the boundaries of which are shown on several maps. Both its present limits and political subdivisions are shown on Map 5-2, page 100. The *City of Toronto* is one of the political subdivisions. The commonly used term *Metro* is an abbreviation of Metropolitan Toronto. The *Metropolitan Toronto Planning Area* (MTPA) contains the Municipality of Metropolitan Toronto and an arc of adjacent municipalities. It is the area over which the Metropolitan Toronto Planning Board has jurisdiction. The Toronto *Census Metropolitan Area* (CMA) includes the area covered by the Metropolitan Toronto Planning Area, except for a small area in the northwest, and extends farther west to take in Oakville and Milton. It is the area that was used as the basis for collecting data about Toronto for both the 1961 and 1966 Census of Canada.

CONTENTS

SECTION 1 IMPRESSIONS OF THE TORONTO LANDSCAPE

Toronto is so large a city that as a rule in this book only one part or one aspect of it will be discussed at any particular time. This presents a problem. When one looks at only a part of something, separate from all the other parts, it is often difficult to see the ways in which all the parts fit together to make up the whole. If, however, one *starts* by examining the whole in a general way, he then has a framework into which he can fit the many separate parts or aspects that he will encounter. For this reason, we have provided the reader with the opportunity to gain some *general* impressions of Toronto before going into detail.

The city as a whole can best be seen by examining the 1968 land use map and the air mosaic photograph of Toronto contained in the envelope at the back of the book. The map shows the extent of the city's built-up area and the major land use patterns. The photograph shows the whole urban area as it appears (except for the colour) from the air.

The materials that follow in this section present some of the more important characteristics of the face of Toronto in a variety of forms, and should deepen many of the impressions gained from the examination of the land use map and the air mosaic.

Focal points

— The characteristics of the appearance of a large city and the things that distinguish a large city from a medium-size or small city
— The size of Toronto compared to other cities
— The degree to which Toronto is over- and under-bounded (The extent of a city can be defined in two ways. First, there is the *corporate* city—in this case Metropolitan Toronto—the extent of which is defined by its political boundary. Second, there is the *geographic* city, which is defined by the extent of its continuous built-up area. When the geographic city extends beyond the political boundary, it is referred to as an *over-bounded* city. When the geographic city does not extend as far as its political boundary, it is referred to as an *under-bounded* city.); the significance of being over- or under-bounded
— Toronto's major functions
— Aspects of living in a large city
— How the many parts of a large city interact or influence one another
— How a large city maintains its links with other places; the degree to which Toronto relies on links with other places
— The principal trends in the development of Toronto; the advantages and disadvantages or problems that the trends might create
— The contrasts that show up in a large city
— Some basic problems that Toronto seems to have
— Likes and dislikes about large cities in general and Toronto in particular

1-1: LOCATION OF TORONTO IN NORTH AMERICA, SHOWING CITIES WITH OVER 1,000,000 POPULATION

1-2: Northwestern limits of Toronto
(assessed population in 1969, 1,935,145)

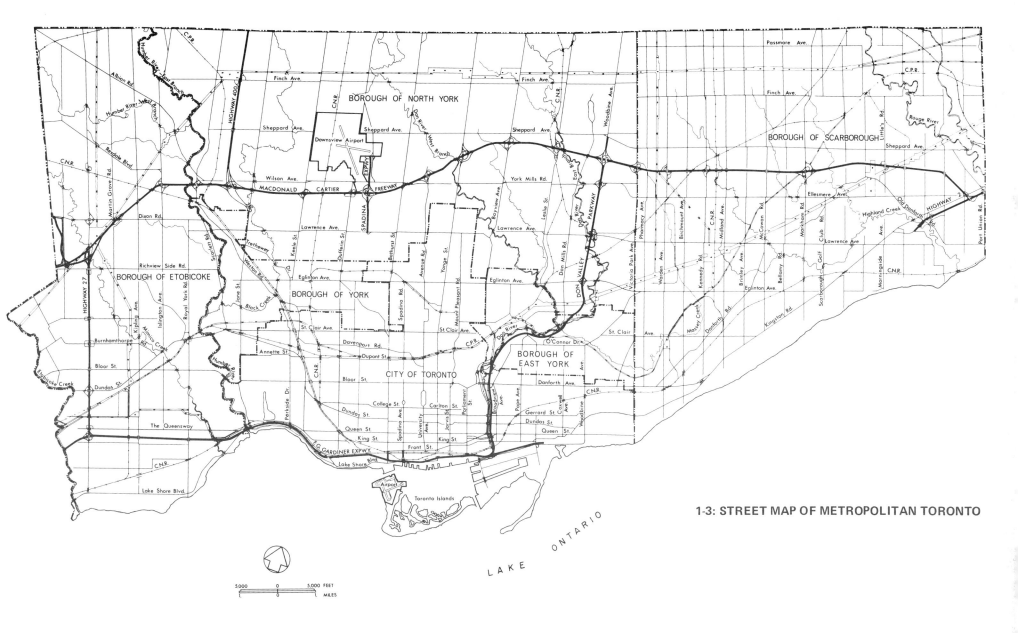

1-3: STREET MAP OF METROPOLITAN TORONTO

BOROUGH OF NORTH YORK

BOROUGH OF SCARBOROUGH

BOROUGH OF ETOBICOKE

BOROUGH OF YORK

CITY OF TORONTO

BOROUGH OF EAST YORK

LAKE ONTARIO

Toronto Islands

5,000   0   5,000 FEET

MILES

3

TORONTO

NEW YORK

LOS ANGELES

WINNIPEG

EDMONTON

MONTREAL

REGINA

LONDON, ENGLAND

VANCOUVER

CHICAGO

A silhouette shows the continuous built-up area of an urban complex and the built-up areas of the principal smaller urban centres located nearby.

Each division in the frames around the silhouettes on this page represents a distance of one mile.

1-4: SELECTED CITY SILHOUETTES

1-5: The symbolic end of Toronto's image as "Hog Town": The Toronto Hog is carried along Bloor Street to its burial, September 1969.

1-6: A study in contrasts—view along Alpha Avenue, looking west

1-9: (top) Leaside industries

1-10: (left) Bloor Street east of Avenue Road

1-11: (top right) The lower Don Valley, looking north

1-12: (top left) The Pickering Nuclear Power Station

1-13: (right) A view from the southwest. Foreground: the Lakeview Thermal Electric Plant

1-14: The Trefann Court Area

1-15: "TORONTO: COULD YOU LIVE THERE?" by Dawn MacDonald

Nobody speaks to them on elevators; they get pushed around in subways, they have trouble finding a place to live, the people at work seem unfriendly. Most of the time, they feel tired and bored and lonely and they want to go home. It's no wonder new Torontonians tend to glorify their past, but it's the first mistake they make.

Toronto is big. With a population of more than two million (one tenth of Canada and one third of Ontario) and a current growth rate of thirty-seven percent per decade, it is one of the fastest-growing cities in North America—and one of the cleanest and safest. Once christened Toronto the Good, the city has about it the expectation that it *is* good, that it *will* have the best educational system, the best transit service, the best planning, the best architecture, and so it tends to lead or compete with the best in the world in all of these categories. Toronto had the advantage of entering the international big-city league after older, cancerous-beyond-hope cities had proved too late the need for imaginative city planning. Famous U.S. urban writer Jane Jacobs (who now lives in Toronto's fashionable downtown Annex area) says that ten years ago, people living in cities all over the Western world caught onto an idea of what a city should be: safe, without racial, occupational, functional or economic ghettoes, with richly variable neighborhood life-styles open to anyone, with a thriving, healthy multifunctional city heart to be used by all citizens, day and night. Cities lacking these qualities became sick, their peoples began to live in fear of one another. Toronto, says Mrs. Jacobs, was lucky. It woke up while it still has something to plan . . . .

Despite the occasional report of rape or murder or street beating, Torontonians do not think of their city as unsafe in comparison with other large cities. City police name two or three streets where it is considered unsafe for a woman to walk and none for a man (compare this with New York where no street is safe for man or woman after dark, where every apartment is double- or triple-padlocked, where every apartment building needs an armed guard). Police claim that warring gangs, once considered the threat to the lone pedestrian, have been completely cleared out of the city. The middle class asserts its firm belief in Toronto's safety by migrating into slum areas (often living one block away from prostitute and drug-addict haunts) to restore old Victorian houses.

Only ten years ago, Toronto was considered one of the dullest, most lifeless places imaginable—but not now. We all know about the changes brought about as the result of the influx of New Canadians in the two decades after World War Two. Three hundred thousand Italians, one hundred thousand Germans and tens of thousands of northern and eastern Europeans swelled the city's population, and by the beginning of the sixties their influence was really felt. Restaurants, music, film, art, architecture, ways of thinking and acting have literally blown Toronto out of its crusty old mold into a bustling, sometimes smug, exciting and stimulating place to be. Because it's a newcomer's city there is a vested interest in change in Toronto, as perhaps in no other Canadian city . . .

Source: *Chatelaine* magazine, May 1970.
Reprinted with permission

SECTION 2 THE SETTING

The conditions of its physical environment and its location in relation to other places have a profound effect on a city.

In this section the characteristics of Toronto's site are presented first. The *site* of a city is that area on which settlement began and over which it has spread. The general physiographic, topographic and climatic aspects of Toronto's site are presented through maps, diagrams, graphs, statistics and newspaper clippings. Following these are photographs showing details of some of the site's most prominent natural features.

After the section dealing with site, there are materials that show some basic aspects of Toronto's situation. The *situation* of a city usually refers to the physical characteristics of a fairly wide area around the settlement. Of equal importance, however, are the human and economic characteristics of the surrounding area and, indeed, of the area considerably beyond this as well. Toronto in relation to its immediate surroundings in South-central Ontario, to Southern Ontario as a whole, and to the highly urbanized and industrialized region of East-central North America can be seen on the maps in this section. A city's situation, of course, is something that shows up in many ways and the materials here do not tell the whole story by any means. In several other places in this book, as well, aspects of Toronto's situation are revealed.

The *setting* of Toronto, then, is a study that embraces both site and situation and it should reveal a great deal about the development of the city.

Focal points
Examination of the materials that follow will make it clear that certain features of the Toronto site deserve special attention. The islands, the harbour, the lakefront, the Lake Plain, the ravines, the shoreline of glacial Lake Iroquois, and the Scarborough Bluffs are very prominent features and have had especially important roles to play in the development of the city. The photos in particular show the details of these features and can be used, together with other resources that may be at your disposal, as bases for an analysis of the geological processes responsible for the formation of the Toronto site.

- The particular aspects of the Toronto site that seem to have had the greatest effects on city development; ways in which the site, itself, has been changed as the city developed
- The influence that site has had on the general form of the city
- The physical, economic and cultural implications of Toronto's location in North America

SITE

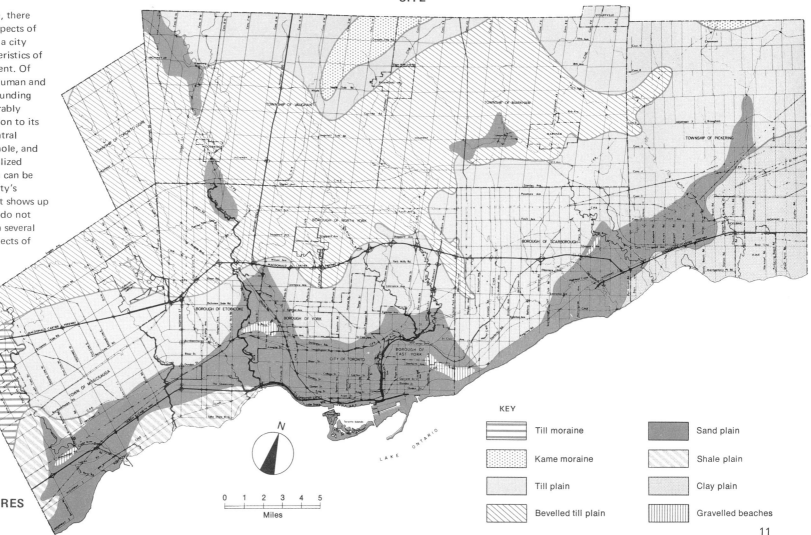

KEY

Till moraine		Sand plain	
Kame moraine		Shale plain	
Till plain		Clay plain	
Bevelled till plain		Gravelled beaches	

0 1 2 3 4 5
Miles

2-1: PHYSIOGRAPHIC FEATURES

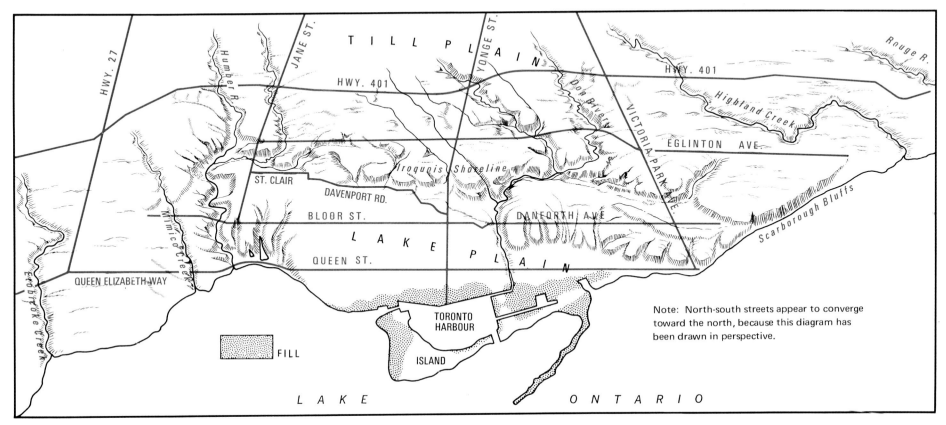

Note: North-south streets appear to converge toward the north, because this diagram has been drawn in perspective.

FILL

2-2: TOPOGRAPHY OF THE METROPOLITAN TORONTO SITE

CROSS-SECTION ALONG YONGE ST. FROM NORTH TO SOUTH *

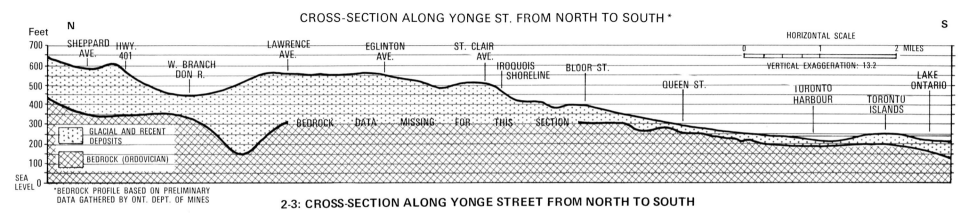

GLACIAL AND RECENT DEPOSITS

BEDROCK (ORDOVICIAN)

*BEDROCK PROFILE BASED ON PRELIMINARY DATA GATHERED BY ONT. DEPT. OF MINES

2-3: CROSS-SECTION ALONG YONGE STREET FROM NORTH TO SOUTH

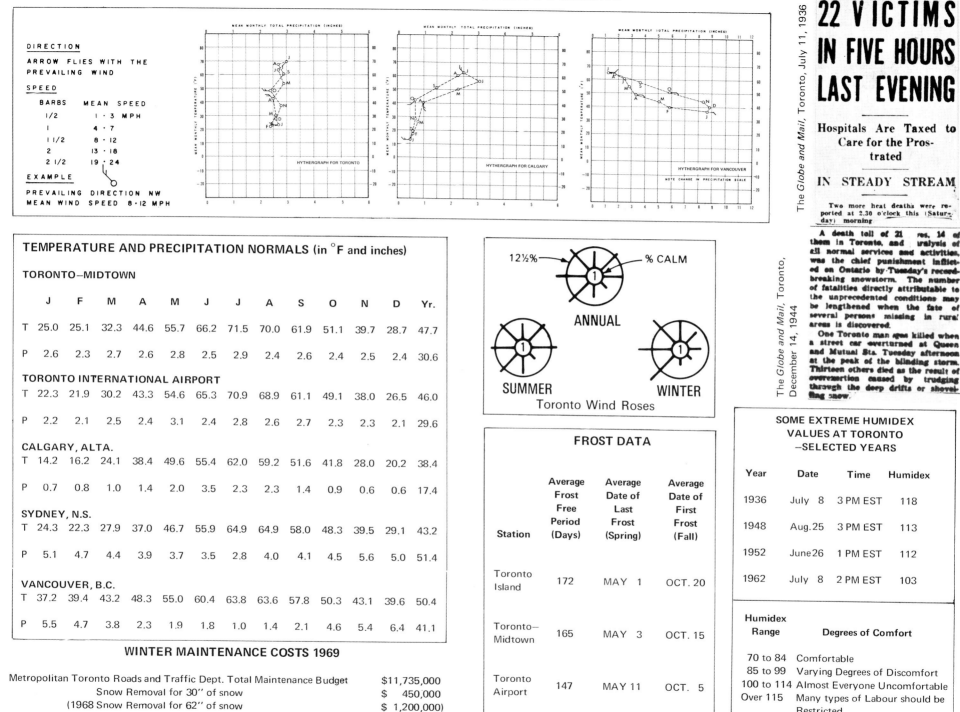

DIRECTION
ARROW FLIES WITH THE PREVAILING WIND

SPEED

BARBS	MEAN SPEED
1/2	1 · 3 MPH
1	4 · 7
1 1/2	8 · 12
2	13 · 18
2 1/2	19 · 24

EXAMPLE
PREVAILING DIRECTION NW
MEAN WIND SPEED 8·12 MPH

HYTHERGRAPH FOR TORONTO

HYTHERGRAPH FOR CALGARY

HYTHERGRAPH FOR VANCOUVER
NOTE CHANGE IN PRECIPITATION SCALE

TEMPERATURE AND PRECIPITATION NORMALS (in °F and inches)

TORONTO—MIDTOWN

	J	F	M	A	M	J	J	A	S	O	N	D	Yr.
T	25.0	25.1	32.3	44.6	55.7	66.2	71.5	70.0	61.9	51.1	39.7	28.7	47.7
P	2.6	2.3	2.7	2.6	2.8	2.5	2.9	2.4	2.6	2.4	2.5	2.4	30.6

TORONTO INTERNATIONAL AIRPORT

	J	F	M	A	M	J	J	A	S	O	N	D	Yr.
T	22.3	21.9	30.2	43.3	54.6	65.3	70.9	68.9	61.1	49.1	38.0	26.5	46.0
P	2.2	2.1	2.5	2.4	3.1	2.4	2.8	2.6	2.7	2.3	2.3	2.1	29.6

CALGARY, ALTA.

	J	F	M	A	M	J	J	A	S	O	N	D	Yr.
T	14.2	16.2	24.1	38.4	49.6	55.4	62.0	59.2	51.6	41.8	28.0	20.2	38.4
P	0.7	0.8	1.0	1.4	2.0	3.5	2.3	2.3	1.4	0.9	0.6	0.6	17.4

SYDNEY, N.S.

	J	F	M	A	M	J	J	A	S	O	N	D	Yr.
T	24.3	22.3	27.9	37.0	46.7	55.9	64.9	64.9	58.0	48.3	39.5	29.1	43.2
P	5.1	4.7	4.4	3.9	3.7	3.5	2.8	4.0	4.1	4.5	5.6	5.0	51.4

VANCOUVER, B.C.

	J	F	M	A	M	J	J	A	S	O	N	D	Yr.
T	37.2	39.4	43.2	48.3	55.0	60.4	63.8	63.6	57.8	50.3	43.1	39.6	50.4
P	5.5	4.7	3.8	2.3	1.9	1.8	1.0	1.4	2.1	4.6	5.4	6.4	41.1

WINTER MAINTENANCE COSTS 1969

Metropolitan Toronto Roads and Traffic Dept. Total Maintenance Budget	$11,735,000
Snow Removal for 30" of snow	$ 450,000
(1968 Snow Removal for 62" of snow	$ 1,200,000)
Salting	$ 2,537,000
Total Winter Maintenance Budget	$ 2,987,000

Source: Metro Roads and Traffic Department

12½% ← | → % CALM

ANNUAL

SUMMER   WINTER

Toronto Wind Roses

FROST DATA

Station	Average Frost Free Period (Days)	Average Date of Last Frost (Spring)	Average Date of First Frost (Fall)
Toronto Island	172	MAY 1	OCT. 20
Toronto—Midtown	165	MAY 3	OCT. 15
Toronto Airport	147	MAY 11	OCT. 5

*Source for all Climatic Data on this page—Meteorological Branch, Department of Transport, Canada

SOME EXTREME HUMIDEX VALUES AT TORONTO —SELECTED YEARS

Year	Date	Time	Humidex
1936	July 8	3 PM EST	118
1948	Aug. 25	3 PM EST	113
1952	June 26	1 PM EST	112
1962	July 8	2 PM EST	103

Humidex Range	Degrees of Comfort
70 to 84	Comfortable
85 to 99	Varying Degrees of Discomfort
100 to 114	Almost Everyone Uncomfortable
Over 115	Many types of Labour should be Restricted

2-5: Scarborough Bluffs
2-6: Scarborough Bluffs. To the north, the Till plain
2-7: The Iroquois shoreline
2-8: A view from the top of the Iroquois shoreline southward along Spadina Avenue
2-9 and 2-10: Exposed bedrock: the lower Humber valley
2-11: Toronto Islands, looking southeast

2-9

2-10

2-11

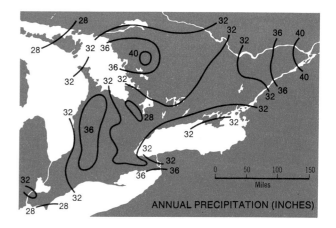

ANNUAL PRECIPITATION (INCHES)

2-12: TOPOGRAPHY: SOUTH-CENTRAL ONTARIO

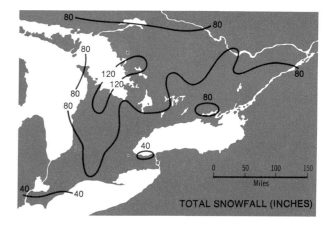

TOTAL SNOWFALL (INCHES)

2-13: TEMPERATURE PATTERNS: SOUTHERN ONTARIO

2-14: PRECIPITATION PATTERNS: SOUTHERN ONTARIO

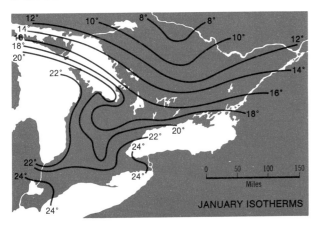

JANUARY ISOTHERMS

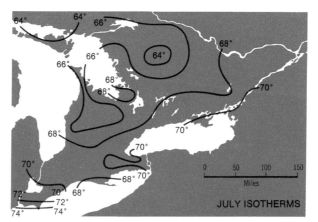

JULY ISOTHERMS

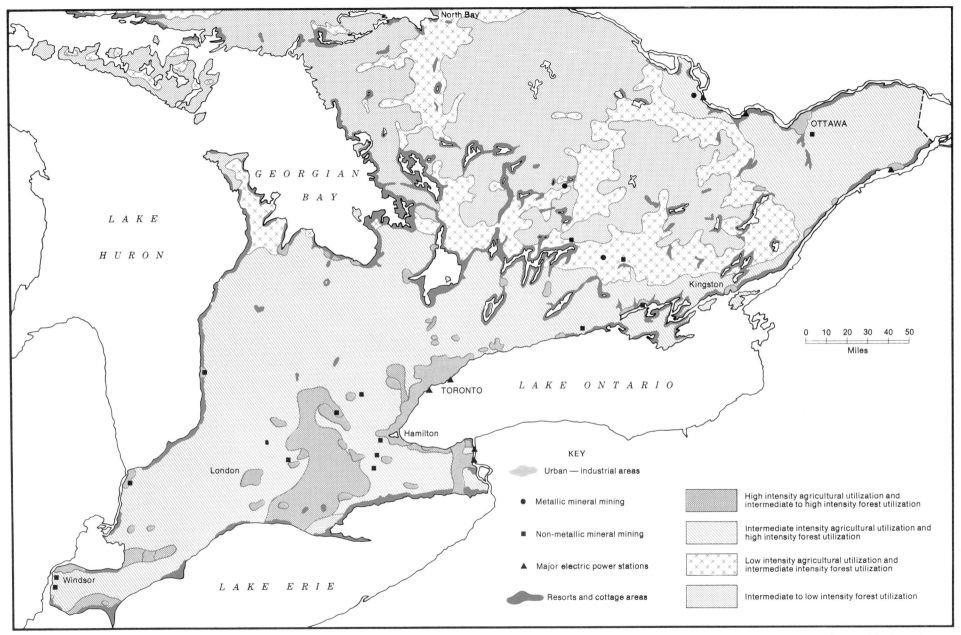

KEY

Urban — industrial areas

● Metallic mineral mining

■ Non-metallic mineral mining

▲ Major electric power stations

Resorts and cottage areas

High intensity agricultural utilization and intermediate to high intensity forest utilization

Intermediate intensity agricultural utilization and high intensity forest utilization

Low intensity agricultural utilization and intermediate intensity forest utilization

Intermediate to low intensity forest utilization

Note: Intensity of agricultural or forest utilization refers to the amount of investment put into the various activities and the amount of production that comes from those activities, not to the areas covered by the activities.

2-15: ECONOMIC LANDSCAPE: SOUTHERN ONTARIO

17

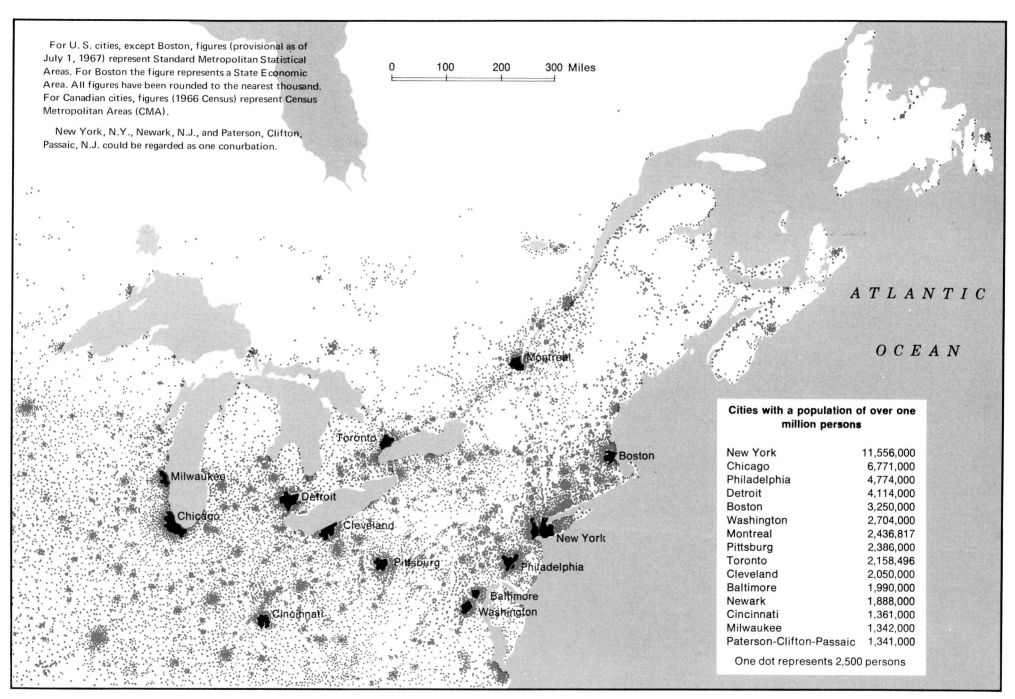

For U.S. cities, except Boston, figures (provisional as of July 1, 1967) represent Standard Metropolitan Statistical Areas. For Boston the figure represents a State Economic Area. All figures have been rounded to the nearest thousand. For Canadian cities, figures (1966 Census) represent Census Metropolitan Areas (CMA).

New York, N.Y., Newark, N.J., and Paterson, Clifton, Passaic, N.J. could be regarded as one conurbation.

0   100   200   300 Miles

ATLANTIC

OCEAN

Montreal

Toronto

Boston

Milwaukee

Detroit

Chicago

Cleveland

Pittsburg

New York

Philadelphia

Baltimore

Cincinnati

Washington

Cities with a population of over one million persons

New York	11,556,000
Chicago	6,771,000
Philadelphia	4,774,000
Detroit	4,114,000
Boston	3,250,000
Washington	2,704,000
Montreal	2,436,817
Pittsburg	2,386,000
Toronto	2,158,496
Cleveland	2,050,000
Baltimore	1,990,000
Newark	1,888,000
Cincinnati	1,361,000
Milwaukee	1,342,000
Paterson-Clifton-Passaic	1,341,000

One dot represents 2,500 persons

2-16: POPULATION: NORTHEASTERN NORTH AMERICA

SECTION 3 THE GROWTH OF TORONTO

Any landscape is the product of a long evolutionary process. A city's landscape evolves under the influence of a complex interplay of many physical, political, economic, cultural, and administrative factors over a considerable period of time. To understand the Toronto of the present, then, we must see it in historical perspective—a perspective that enables us to trace the roots and follow the development of the various aspects of the city that characterize it today.

The materials that follow are numerous and varied. There are copies of some of the original maps drawn by early surveyors. Among the pictures are several artists' impressions of the city and these provide remarkably useful evidence of the nature of the city's landscape at key stages in its history. Land use maps of the late nineteenth-century city and the early Second World War city are also provided and can be used as a basis for interesting comparisons and contrasts with the pattern of today. Selected newspaper clippings reflect the processes by which Toronto rose to commercial prominence in the nineteenth century. Finally, since a study that deals with growth needs continuity, an historical narrative has been included.

Focal points
— The factors that influenced the location of settlements on the Toronto site in the early stages of its development
— The directions in which the city spread (or the lines of thrust) during the nineteenth and twentieth centuries
— The following aspects of the city at various stages in its development
  form (the general shape of a city)
  general appearance
  architecture
  functions
  land use patterns
  modes of transportation
  city life
  relationship to hinterland
— names—past and present
— The aspects of the past that survive in some form today; the aspects of the past that have completely disappeared
— The roles the following factors played in Toronto's rise to metropolitan status
  political and administrative decisions
  national and international events
  site and situation
  advances in technology

1. THE BEGINNINGS

Toronto Carrying-Place, Teiaiagon, and Ganatsekwyagon

Early in the exploration of Canada, when travel into the interior was by canoe and trail, a route was developed that crossed the Ontario peninsula from the western end of Lake Ontario to Georgian Bay. This route quickly became a vital link in the fur trade of the Great Lakes-St. Lawrence region. It saved the traveller who was proceeding from Lake Ontario to the upper lakes a detour of hundreds of miles that would have required his sailing across Lake Erie, through the Detroit River-Lake St. Clair-St. Clair River system and up the long stretch of Lake Huron. The southern 30 miles of the new short-cut consisted of a low and fairly easy portage that ran from the mouth of what is now called the Humber River, up the Humber valley to the west branch of the Holland River. This portage became known as the *Toronto Carrying-Place.* (The name Toronto may well have come from the Huron word for pass or gate which took two forms, *karontaen* and *tarontaen.*) Once the traveller reached the northern end of the portage, he could proceed along the Holland River, into Lake Simcoe and eventually into Georgian Bay. A second trail led from the mouth of the Rouge River, twenty miles to the east of the Humber, to the east branch of the Holland River. Both routes from Lake Ontario to Georgian Bay became known as the *Toronto Passage.* The small Seneca village of Teiaiagon was established near the mouth of the Humber; Ganatsekwyagon was established at the mouth of the Rouge. Being at the southern end of the Toronto Carrying-Place, both villages became important centres for the fur trade.

The French Period

In the middle of the seventeenth century, the Iroquois controlled almost the entire area of what is today Southern Ontario and had developed an active fur trade with the English, Dutch, and Swedes who were concentrated to their southeast in the Hudson valley and the New Jersey area. The French, in an attempt to capture the fur trade from the Iroquois and their English and Dutch allies, began exploring and developing bases in the Lake Ontario region. For the first time, French settlement began to move westward from the banks of the St. Lawrence. Moreover, by this time, France had conceived a new role for itself in North America. It was to become an empire builder and to extend its domain west and south to the valley of the Mississippi. The Toronto Carrying-Place or *le passage de Toronto* thus became not only a short-cut between Lake Ontario and the upper lakes but part of one of the principal highways to the Mississippi.

During the first half of the eighteenth century, the English position in North America grew steadily stronger. A symbol of the growing tension between the English and French over control of the fur trade in the Lake Ontario region was Fort Toronto, which the French erected on the banks of the Humber in 1750. A second and larger fort, known both as Fort Rouillé and Fort Toronto, was completed three miles to the east of the first Fort Toronto in 1751. Hostilities between the English and French came to a head when war was declared in 1756. In 1759, when it became apparent that their post at Niagara, only a short distance from Toronto, would fall to the English, the French burned Fort Rouillé.

The Founding of York

On August 1, 1788, the HMS *Seneca,* with 18 mounted guns and carrying a crew of 35 and a survey party, entered Toronto harbour. In her hold were gifts and provisions for the Mississauga Indians who were about to assemble at Toronto. A few days later a second ship arrived from Niagara, carrying Lord Dorchester, Governor-General of Canada, and several other British officials. The occasion

was the completion of the Toronto Purchase— the selling of a large tract of land at Toronto by the Mississaugas to the British.

Lord Dorchester was well aware of just how strategic the site at the foot of the Toronto Carrying-Place had become. With the cession of the territory south of the Great Lakes to the United States after the American War of Independence, the region northwest of the lakes was more important to the fur trade than ever before and the Toronto portage, therefore, became a link of increased value.

There were only a few scattered inhabitants in the Toronto area at the time of the purchase. Surrounding the 300 acres of abandoned cleared ground around the ruins of old Fort Rouillé was a dense and trackless forest. Swamps were scattered across the Lake Plain; meadows flanked the lower Don. The peninsula, which was later to become the Toronto Islands of today, was clothed in pines, willows and poplars, and wild fowl abounded in the marshes that had formed in the lagoons.

A few days after the transaction had been completed, Alexander Aitkin, on instructions from the Deputy Surveyor-General, carried out a survey of the purchased land and erected a store-house to shelter the gifts and provisions.

In 1791 the British Government passed the Constitutional Act which divided the province of Quebec into the English-speaking province of Upper Canada in the west, and the mainly French-speaking province of Lower Canada in the east. John Graves Simcoe was appointed Upper Canada's first Lieutenant-Governor. After making a careful study of the geography of his new province, Simcoe formulated a comprehensive master plan for the development of Upper Canada's resources and the creation of an effective defence system. He was convinced that the Toronto area afforded the best opportunities for the establishment of a major military base and commercial centre. Even though the fur trade preferred the St. Lawrence-Ottawa Valley route to the west, Simcoe was optimistic about the possibilities of greatly increased trade through the Toronto Passage. Furthermore, with its easily defended harbour, dense stands of excellent timber, and its location a considerable distance from the United States border, Toronto was in his words

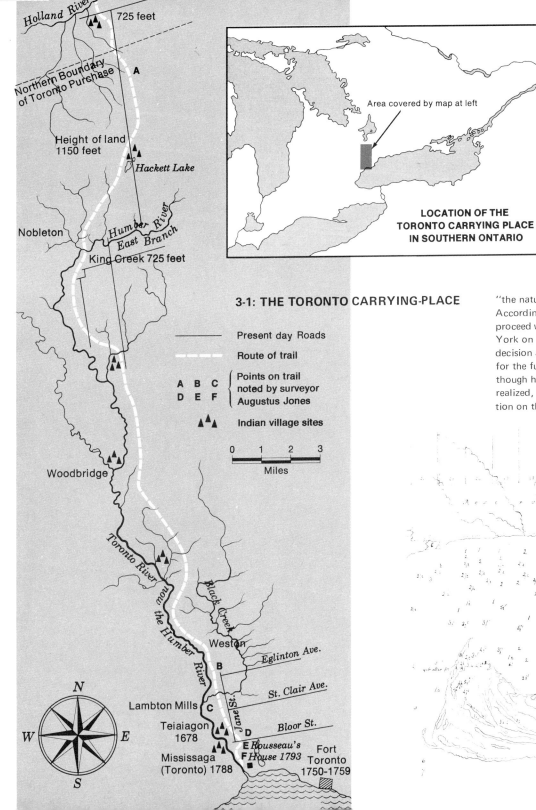

3-1: THE TORONTO CARRYING-PLACE

Holland River

725 feet

Northern Boundary of Toronto Purchase

A

Height of land 1150 feet

Hackett Lake

Nobleton

Humber River East Branch

King Creek 725 feet

Woodbridge

Toronto River or mouth the Humber River

Black Creek

Weston

Eglinton Ave.

B

St. Clair Ave.

Jane St.

Lambton Mills

C

Teiaiagon 1678

Bloor St.

D

E Rousseau's
F House 1793

Mississaga (Toronto) 1788

Fort Toronto 1750-1759

Present day Roads

Route of trail

A B C D E F Points on trail noted by surveyor Augustus Jones

▲▲▲ Indian village sites

0 1 2 3
Miles

N E S W

LOCATION OF THE TORONTO CARRYING PLACE IN SOUTHERN ONTARIO

Area covered by map at left

"the natural arsenal of Lake Ontario." Accordingly, in 1793, Simcoe decided to proceed with the building of the town of York on the Toronto site. It was a bold decision and a decision of great importance for the future of Toronto, because, even though his plans for a military base were never realized, Simcoe succeeded in focussing attention on the possibilities of establishing a major commercial centre at the foot of the Toronto Passage.

Alexander Aitkin was charged for the second time with the responsibility of drawing up a street plan. This time, however, instead of fronting on the central part of the bay, the town site was to be situated farther east, near the mouth of the Don. The plan set out the streets in the traditional, unimaginative European grid—a network that, as it was extended, would soon come into conflict with the topography of the Toronto site. Nevertheless, from its beginning, York was a planned town.

Simcoe's enthusiasm for the military possibilities of York was not shared by Governor Dorchester who refused to approve or grant funds for most of Simcoe's plans. As a result, York never became the arsenal that Simcoe hoped it would. Simcoe's plans for York were not entirely curbed, however. He laid out the new townsite and managed to complete the construction of Yonge Street for military communication in 1796. Situated several miles to the east of the old trail up the

3-2: AITKIN'S PLAN OF YORK, 1793

PLAN of YORK HARBOUR
Surveyed by order of L.t Gov.t Simcoe
by A. Aitkin

ONTARIO

LAKE

References
A Proposed Block House to Command the mouth of the Harbour
B Proposed Battery
C Proposed Barracks, the lines show disposition of ground for the Queens Rangers
D City of York
E Point from whence the View is taken

Humber valley, the new road extended northward some 34 miles from York to Holland Landing on the Holland River. Yonge Street stimulated settlement in the York region and helped to foster the growth of the town's agricultural hinterland.

Even though he minimized the importance of York as a military base, Dorchester made it the capital of Upper Canada in 1794. In doing so he laid a foundation for the growth of the town that was to prove enormously beneficial. York's inaccessibility (the nearest non-Indian settlements were at Niagara, 75 miles away, and Kingston, 180 miles away) necessitated the building of roads that would converge on the new capital, thus making it the principal focus of land routes in Upper Canada. Lot Street (later Queen Street) was extended westward to join the Dundas Highway to Niagara and eastward to Kingston as the Kingston Road.

At the end of the eighteenth century, York had a population of some 300. King and George Streets were the first streets completed as part of the Aitkin plan. Thirty-four park lots of 100 acres each, used for farms, summer residences, and country estates for York's leading citizens, were laid out north of Lot Street. Front Street roughly followed the shoreline and the town enjoyed a close association with the harbour and lake.

In 1797 a new townsite, with larger blocks, was laid out to the west of the old one. The land between the old and new towns was reserved for public buildings such as the hospital, school, jail, church, and market.

3-3: York, the capital of Upper Canada, 1804

2. THE NINETEENTH CENTURY: TORONTO'S RISE TO COMMERCIAL PROMINENCE

Background: 1800-1850

The early years of the nineteenth century were not especially promising years for York. It was remote from the other centres of the colony and, at first, not even its function as capital did much to promote growth. During the War of 1812 between Canada and the United States, the town suffered considerable destruction at the hands of American invaders. By 1815, however, it was on the threshold of an era of progress and development that was to see it rise from a backwoods village to the status of a metropolis.*

Dorchester's selection of York as capital meant, of course, that the government officials of the old capital of Newark (now Niagara-on-the-Lake) were required to move and take up residence in the new settlement. In compensation for their losses of property in Newark, they were given generous grants of land in the York area. As York prospered, this élite group, who came to be known as the Family Compact, soon realized that their own fortunes were strongly tied to those of the town itself. Several members of the group developed strong business interests in the York area. This close relationship between business and politics, started in York, grew to become one of the features of life in Upper Canada. The efforts of the élite to develop the commercial potential of the capital profoundly affected its growth for the next several decades. In the establishment of the Bank of Upper Canada in York in 1822, for example, 4 of the 15 directors were appointed by the government and 12 of them were members of the Family Compact. Moreover, this group succeeded in influencing the Government to deny all further petitions to establish banks in Upper Canada, thus giving the new York-based bank a clear advantage. Kingston, with three banks, was still the economic heart of Upper Canada, but it in time suffered from its financial dependence on Montreal. York, on the other hand, much farther from Montreal, enjoyed an independent growth and soon outstripped Kingston as Upper Canada's principal centre of trade and finance.

On March 4, 1834, the Town of York, with a population of 9,256, became the City of Toronto, with William Lyon Mackenzie as its first mayor.

The first half of the nineteenth century also witnessed a great improvement in Toronto's continental trade situation. The Erie Canal was opened in 1825, linking the Great Lakes to New York City. Its Oswego extension was completed three years later. This route gave Toronto an outlet to the Atlantic that by-passed Montreal and provided better navigational conditions than those of the St. Lawrence system. The Drawback Act, passed in 1846 in the United States, allowed the free movement of goods to Upper Canada via the port of New York. Upper Canada dealers, seeing the obvious advantages of the Toronto-New York route for importing and exporting, began to concentrate their activities in Toronto, and wholesale trade flourished in the city. Toronto was thus able to expand its hinterland at the expense of Montreal, which suffered a serious loss of North American trade.

By mid-century, Toronto was the centre of the best road network in the province, had become the prime commercial city for an extensive area north and west of Lake Ontario, and had begun to organize the import-export market of its growing hinterland—a hinterland that awaited the development of the railway for further extension.

The Face of the City, 1800-1850

By 1850, Toronto had begun to assume its characteristic form. The original townsite, surveyed by Aitkin, had long ceased to be the centre of the city. The tendency to spread westward that had begun with the laying out of the new town in 1797 was now a well-

---

* On page 99, a hypothesis of city growth advanced by Professor N. S. B. Gras is outlined. He recognized four basic stages through which a city passes in its rise to metropolitan status. It is interesting to keep these stages in mind while examining the materials and narrative of this section to see how closely the Toronto case parallels the Gras hypothesis.

established trend. There were five major reasons for this direction of growth. First, the land on the eastern margins of the original townsite was swampy and difficult to build on; north of this area and east of Yonge Street expansion was limited by Taddle Creek. Second, two important buildings were located in the western part of the site: old Fort York, and, after 1828, the provincial parliament buildings. Third, Yonge Street had become the chief land route to the northern hinterland.

Fourth, a pleasant lakeshore stretched toward the garrison in the west (prominent citizens built their residences along Front Street early in the development of the town). Fifth, Lot Street (Queen Street) exerted a considerable pull as the principal route to the western hinterland.

The commercial heart of the city developed along King Street between Bay Street and George Street. The centre of early York life, however, revolved around two foci: the City Hall and Market in the old eastern section, and the centre of government in the newer western section.

Subdivision of the area east of Parliament Street started in the 1830's and proceeded on an ill-planned, piece by piece basis. Small houses were crowded into the city blocks, especially south of Gerrard Street. This area became the famous Cabbagetown neighbourhood, so-called because the early residents were in the habit of planting cabbages in every available plot of ground—even their front yards—in order to feed themselves.

With their fine view of the bay from the public mall built along the shore, and the availability of large tracts of undeveloped land north of Queen Street, the townsfolk felt no need to set aside areas of parkland in the town itself. The absence of open-space areas in downtown Toronto today can be attributed, in large part, to this former shortsightedness.

There were, however, occasional examples of imagination and concern for the future. The Baldwin family were responsible for the development of Spadina Avenue into a street of unusual width, as befitted a thoroughfare that led to their large estate. Two parallel roads that extended along the edges of adjacent parklots were joined to give University Avenue its impressive width.

By the 1840's Toronto had begun to cut its close association with the bay. With the city's continuing growth as a major port, and the development of larger vessels, wharves had to be extended, and more and more land was reclaimed along the waterfront. Public land disappeared as businesses crowded into the waterfront area. A decade later the situation was aggravated by the building of railways.

The Census of 1851 revealed the following ethnic breakdown of the city's 30,775 residents:

English	4,958
Scottish	2,169
Irish	11,305
Canadians of non-French origin	9,856
French origin	467
Americans	1,405
Others	515

There were three distinct classes in Toronto society at that time: the older-established aristocracy (members of the Family Compact), the newer business class, and everybody else. The first two classes formed the basis of what became the famous Toronto Tory group, a group not united by political principle alone but also by a definite attitude of mind. It was an Anglo-Saxon group which strongly supported the British Empire and the Monarchy and stood squarely against Roman Catholicism. It was also decidedly anti-American. The members of this group were the original Toronto WASPS.*

The militant Protestantism of this group had a strong effect on the political, economic, and social development of Toronto. The Tory predominated in politics. The typical Protestant businessman was a plain-living, God-fearing, hard-working soul whose religion gave sanction to vigorous commercial enterprise. By 1850 the city had 24 churches and the image of "Toronto the Good" had begun to form.

A visitor's impression of the city in the 1840's is afforded by this interesting description by Charles Dickens. "The country around this town being very flat is bare of scenic interest, but the town itself is full of life and motion, bustle, business and improvement. The streets are well paved and lighted with gas; the houses are large and good; the shops excellent. Many of them have a display in their windows such as may be seen in thriving country towns of England, and there are some which would do no discredit to the metropolis itself. There is a good stone prison here; and there are, besides, a handsome church, a court house, public offices, many commodious private residences, and a Government Observatory for noting and recording the magnetic variations. In the College of Upper Canada, which is one of the public establishments of the city, a sound education in every department of polite learning can be had at very moderate expense, the annual charge for the instruction of each pupil not exceeding nine pounds sterling."

* A commonly used contraction of the words White Anglo-Saxon Protestant

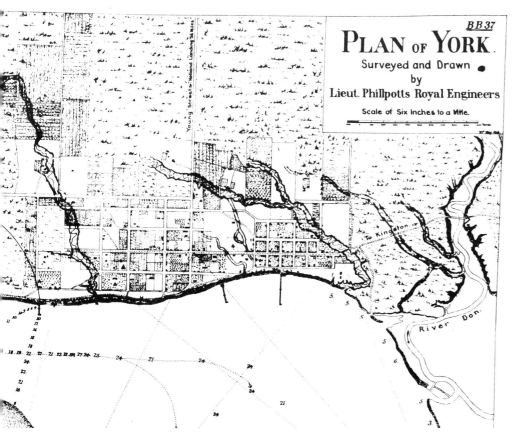

3-4: PHILPOTTS' PLAN OF YORK, CIRCA 1818

PLAN OF YORK.
BB 37
Surveyed and Drawn
by
Lieut. Phillpotts Royal Engineers
Scale of Six Inches to a Mile.

3-5: Köllner's view of Toronto, circa 1840

3-6: Looking eastward along King Street, 1836

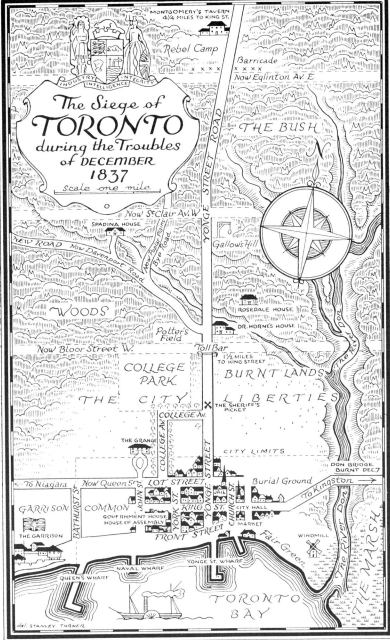

3-7: TORONTO AND THE AREA IMMEDIATELY NORTH, 1837

3-8: Toronto in 1834: Whitefield's view, looking westward along Front Street

DARLING BROTHERS,

WHOLESALE IMPORTERS,

KING STREET.

(Opposite the ruins of the old Cathedral.)

HAVE at present on hand, a large assortment of HARDWARE, STATIONERY, and FANCY GOODS, which they will sell on liberal terms and to which they would call the attention of country merchants.

Toronto, 15th March, 1850.　　527-tf

NOTICE TO SPECULATORS.

THE Subscriber will contract to deliver at any Port in North America, 300 barrels of superior OATMEAL.

ROBT. ANDERSON.

Nitavale Mills,
　Ayr, Dumfries
　　March 4, 1850.　　524-tf

April 4, 1850

NEW LINE OF STEAMERS

Between Montreal and Toronto and Hamilton!

THE Subscribers, having completed arrangements for running a regular *Line of first-class Steamers* between Montreal and Toronto and Hamilton, calling at other ports on Lake Ontario, will be prepared, on the opening of Navigation, to transport goods and produce, *without transhipment* on the most favourable terms.

They have also made arrangements to run a Line of

FIRST-CLASS BARGES,

(In addition to their old established line of Steamers and Barges on the River St. Lawrence) from Kingston and Montreal direct to Lake Champlain and are prepared to contract for the transportation of produce from ports on Lakes Erie and Ontario to Burlington and other ports on Lake Champlain.

HOOKER & HOLTON.

Montreal, March 1, 1850.　　521-3m

April 30, 1850

THE Subscriber having rented from the City Corporation, in the West Wing of the New Market Buildings, commodious *STORAGE and OFFICE ROOM,* is now ready to receive on Consignment all descriptions of

Goods, Wares and Merchandize,

in bond or otherwise; as also to purchase, store and ship all kinds of Grain, Seed, Flour, and Meal, &c. &c. &c.

Prompt attention will be given to effect Sales, and net proceeds transmitted to order with punctuality and despatch. A thorough knowledge of mercantile transactions, and some years of practical experience in the trade in Canada West, are guarantees to parties at a distance, who may feel disposed to avail themselves of the Trade of Toronto.

Reference.—John Tracey, Esq., Merchant, Albany; Robert Codd, Esq., Banker, Buffalo; Messrs. Wood & Grant, Merchants, New York.

JAMES FITZGERALD,
Commission Merchant and Agent.

Toronto, Dec. 6th, 1849.

SUPERFINE FLOUR for family use, for Sale in Barrels.

JAMES FITZGERALD.

OFFICES TO LET.

A FEW Offices, in a desirable locality.

JAMES FITZGERALD.

Toronto, Dec. 6, 1849.　　484-tf-T

April 16, 1850

Advances on Produce consigned to New York.

THE Undersigned are prepared to make *liberal advances* to parties consigning Produce for Sale to Messrs. HIGGINSON, DAY & Co., of New York.

HUTCHINSON, BLACK & Co.

Toronto, March 5th, 1850.　　523-tf

NOTICE TO SPECULATORS.

THE Subscriber will contract to deliver at any Port in North America, 300 barrels of superior OATMEAL.

ROBT. ANDERSON.

Nithvale Mills,
　Ayr, Dumfries
　　March 4, 1850.　　524-tf

May 2, 1850
Used with permission of The *Globe and Mail,* Toronto

Background: 1850-1900

The first great period of railway development began in the 1850's. In 1852 tracks were being laid for the Ontario Simcoe and Huron Railway from Toronto to Bradford some 40 miles to the north. In 1856 the Grand Trunk was completed, linking Toronto and Montreal. The spread of the rail net expanded Toronto's hinterland northward and westward to Georgian Bay, the Canadian Shield, and eventually to the far west. The growth of railways greatly heightened the rivalry between Toronto and Montreal for the trade of the vast Canadian interior.

At the beginning of the railway era Toronto was still far behind Montreal in its financial function. But Toronto's trading position continued to improve. With the construction of more roads and railways, the city became a major focus of routes. Farmers in Southern Ontario enjoyed better access to the city and Toronto merchants catered more and more to the wants of the country merchants: city and hinterland became mutually dependent and closely tied to each other. Firms from outside the city began to transfer their businesses to Toronto. Timothy Eaton arrived in 1868 to establish a store that would become a household name in Canada. In 1879 the Massey-Harris farm implement company moved in from Newcastle, a small town 40 miles to the east.

Toronto was soon to become the jumping-off point for northern development as well. The lumber industry pushed northward into Muskoka and there was a growing awareness of the importance of the mineral resources of the Canadian Shield.

By 1870 Toronto had become a mercantile centre of considerable strength but it was *still* far less important than Montreal in the world of finance. In 1871, however, an event took place which was to prove of immense value to Toronto-based banks. The passing of the Bank Act provided legislation that brought to an end the control of the financial matters of the country that had been held for so long by the Bank of Montreal and paved the way for the rise of Toronto as Canada's leading financial centre.

The city also was growing rapidly as a manufacturing centre. In 1881 it had 932 industries employing 13,245 workers. Ten years later 2,401 industries employed 26,242 workers.

By 1890 Toronto's population had risen to 181,220, partly through the annexation of several suburban communities such as Parkdale to the west and Yorkville to the north, but chiefly as a result of the tremendous growth it experienced in the decade of the eighties. The city was on the verge of becoming a metropolis.

The Face of the City, 1850-1900

The second half of the nineteenth century saw many changes in the face of Toronto.

In April of 1858 a severe storm slashed through the neck of land that formed the southern and eastern side of the bay and created the eastern gap. In the 1880's, the lower Don was straightened to allow the CPR access to the waterfront from the east.

Map 3-14 (p. 31), showing the original settlements, indicates the existence of several suburban communities which, through a process of annexation that began in 1883, were absorbed by the city. Surviving buildings and land use patterns in these communities lend a distinctive personality to many parts of the metropolitan area today.

Map 3-14 also shows several important aspects of the city's form at that time. The shoreline of glacial Lake Iroquois, it is interesting to note, still provided an effective barrier to northward development. The central business district had expanded considerably westward and Yonge Street had become the leading commercial street. The city's industries and warehouses were concentrated along the railways. Fashionable houses were found along Jarvis Street and in the outlying neighbourhoods of Rosedale and Parkdale; the lowest class residences were adjacent to the retail core. High class or low class, however, Toronto had become a city of homeowners.

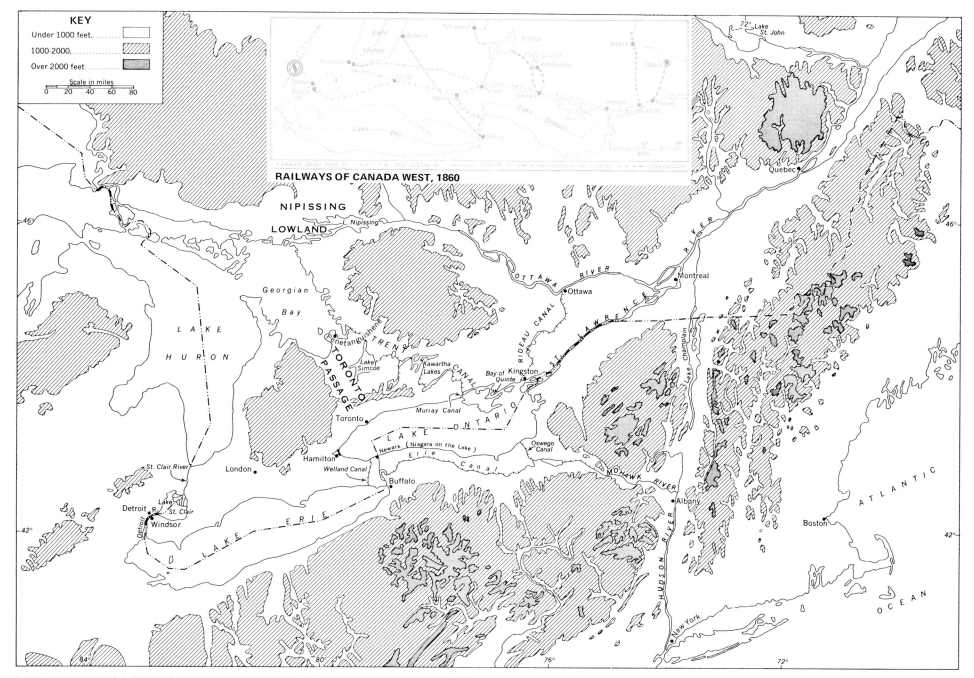

KEY

Under 1000 feet ....
1000-2000, ...
Over 2000 feet ....

Scale in miles
0 20 40 60 80

RAILWAYS OF CANADA WEST, 1860

NIPISSING

LOWLAND

L. Nipissing

Georgian

Bay

L A K E

H U R O N

Penetanguishene

Lake Simcoe

Kawartha Lakes

TRENT

CANAL

Murray Canal

TORONTO PASSAGE

Toronto

Bay of Quinte

Kingston

RIDEAU CANAL

ST. LAWRENCE

OTTAWA   RIVER

Ottawa

Montreal

RIVER

Quebec

Lake St. John

L A K E   O N T A R I O

Newark (Niagara on the Lake)

Oswego Canal

Hamilton

Erie   Canal

London

Welland Canal

Buffalo

MOHAWK   RIVER

Lake Champlain

St. Clair River

Detroit R.   Lake St. Clair

Detroit

Windsor

Detroit

L A K E   E R I E

Albany

HUDSON   RIVER

A T L A N T I C

Boston

New York

O C E A N

72°

46°

46°

42°

42°

84°

80°

76°

72°

3-10: TORONTO'S LOCATION WITH RESPECT TO MAIN TRANSPORTATION ROUTES, IN THE MID-NINETEENTH CENTURY

3-11: PART OF TREMAINE'S MAP, 1860

3-12: Gascard's view of Toronto, circa 1873

KEY

1. Northern Railway Shops
2. Northern Railway Offices
3. Knox College, Spadina Avenue (now the Connaught Laboratory, University of Toronto)
4. University of Toronto
5. St. George's Church
6. St. Patrick's Church
7. Foot of Windsor Street (now railway freight yards)
8. Grand Trunk Round House on Esplanade
9. Toronto Water Works
10. John Street

11. Government House
12. Parliament Buildings
13. Osgoode Hall
14. St. Michael's Cathedral
15. Metropolitan Church
16. Union Station
17. St. James' Cathedral
18. St. Lawrence Hall
19. Old City Hall
20. Old Great Western Station
21. Yonge Street Wharf
22. York Street Wharf
23. Grand Trunk Railway Elevator

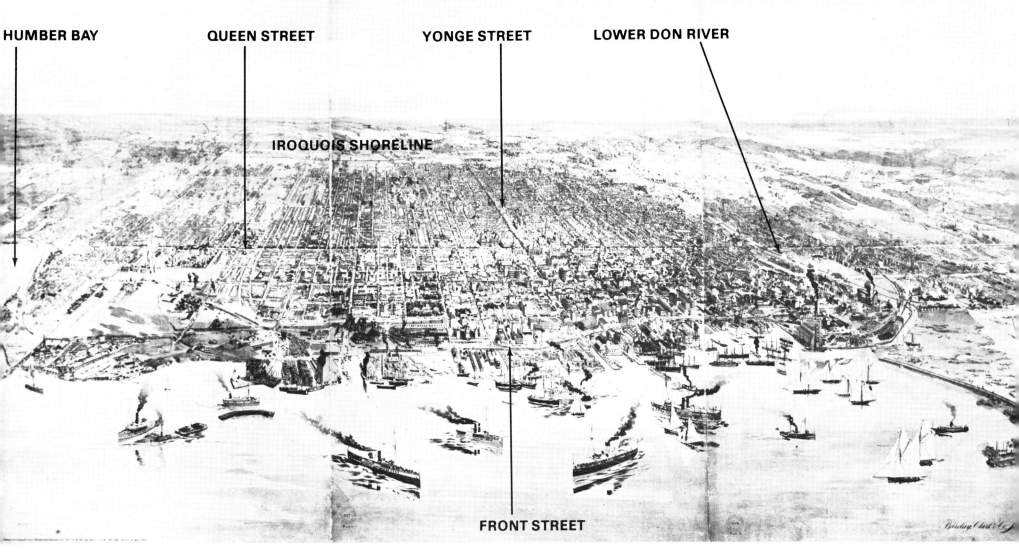

HUMBER BAY   QUEEN STREET   YONGE STREET   LOWER DON RIVER

IROQUOIS SHORELINE

FRONT STREET

3-13 Owen Staples' view of Toronto, 1897

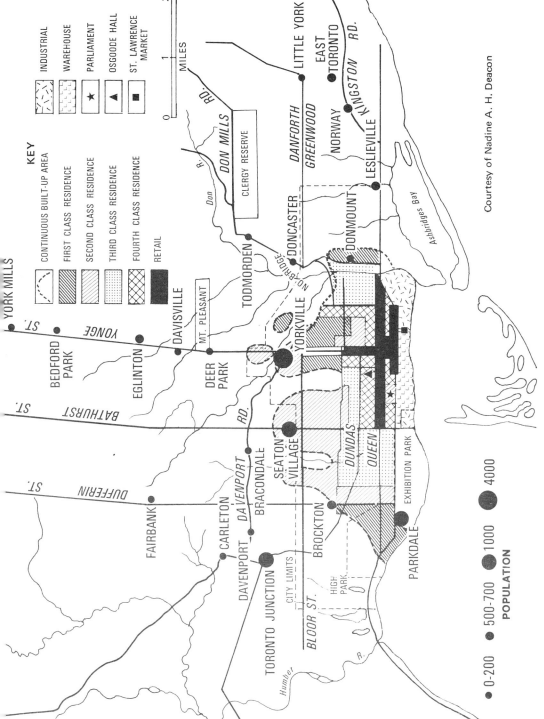

KEY

INDUSTRIAL
WAREHOUSE
PARLIAMENT ★
OSGOODE HALL ▲
ST. LAWRENCE MARKET ■

CONTINUOUS BUILT-UP AREA
FIRST CLASS RESIDENCE
SECOND CLASS RESIDENCE
THIRD CLASS RESIDENCE
FOURTH CLASS RESIDENCE
RETAIL

POPULATION

● 0-200
● 500-700
● 1000
● 4000

Courtesy of Nadine A. H. Deacon

3-14: LAND USE 1885, AND ORIGINAL SETTLEMENTS, 1878

Courtesy Art Gallery of Ontario

3-15: Lower Yonge Street in 1890

31

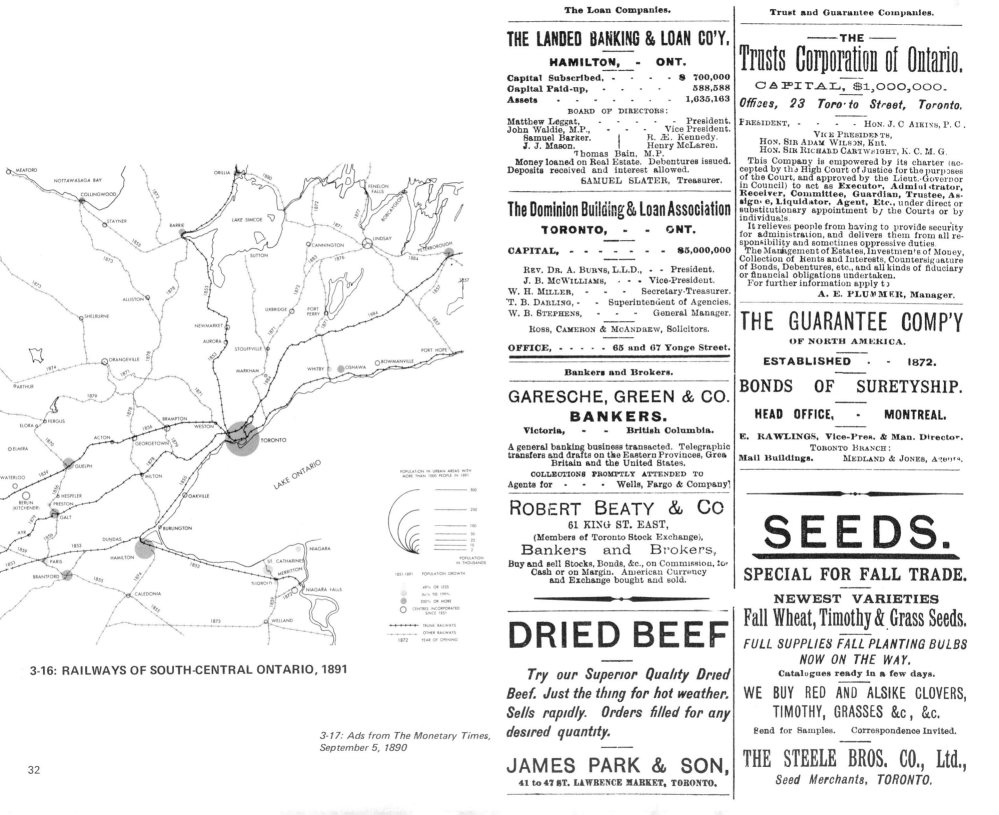

3-16: RAILWAYS OF SOUTH-CENTRAL ONTARIO, 1891

3-17: Ads from The Monetary Times, September 5, 1890

32

3-18: Bay Street, immediately south of Queen Street, decorated in preparation for the visit of the Duke of York (later King George V) in 1901

3-19: The west side of Yonge Street, between Queen and Albert Streets, in 1872. Eleven years later, Timothy Eaton was to establish a new store at 194 Yonge Street, shown in this photo.

3-20: Part of Toronto's waterfront in the 1870's, showing the tower of St. Lawrence Hall and, immediately in front of it, the old City Hall. For much of the nineteenth century this area was the centre of city life.

3-21: William Lyon Mackenzie's house on Bond Street, built circa 1850. Mackenzie was Toronto's first mayor, and leader of the Rebellion of 1837.

3. THE TWENTIETH-CENTURY METROPOLIS .

Background: 1900-1945

Toronto reached metropolitan status in the early decades of the twentieth century. By 1914, 11 railways converged on the city and it had become the undisputed trade, industrial and financial capital of most of Ontario. (It soon was widely referred to as "Hog Town"— a nickname bestowed on it not only because of its economic dominance and disproportionately high share of wealth, but because it was to many an unexciting and colourless place, devoid of any "big city" sophistication.) It did not, however, become the major railway centre it had hoped to become. The CPR transcontinental line was laid from Montreal through the Ottawa valley and thence north-westward across the vast Ontario northland to the west. Toronto, once again, was in a marginal position compared to its long-standing rival. Important links from Toronto to the transcontinental system were soon constructed, however, and the city was able to maintain its position as a major focus of routes.

After the discovery of important mineral deposits in the Cobalt, Kirkland Lake, and Porcupine (Timmins) areas, the Temiskaming and Northern Ontario Railway was built north-ward from North Bay, and Toronto became the principal base for men and equipment destined for the mining regions. Indeed, development of northern resources was a major broadening factor in the growth of Toronto's financial institutions. In 1925 the Northern Ontario Building was erected on Bay Street, symboliz-ing the strong role the city played in northern development.

Manufacturing continued to prosper in what, by the turn of the century, could be called the industrial city. With the development of new manufacturing techniques, larger plants were built. As money, labour and markets were concentrated more and more in the few larger cities of Ontario, there was a general decline of manufacturing in the smaller towns and cities and Toronto's prominence as a manu-facturing centre thus continued to grow.

The city was also developing into an administrative centre of national and inter-national importance. In 1933, for example, 25 out of 52 major Canadian mining companies had located their head offices in Toronto.

The Face of the City, 1900-1945

According to one theory of city growth* a city goes through three distinct phases as it expands:

1. It grows from the centre of origin in widening concentric zones, each of which has a characteristic general land use pattern.
2. The city extends its political limits by annexation.
3. There is a lateral expansion of the built-up area and a vertical growth in the centre of the city.

By the end of the First World War, Toronto was into the third phase in its central business district. Skyscrapers had begun to appear, land values were soaring and there was a general lack of room for expansion. Lateral expansion of the built-up area beyond the downtown core continued along the main lines of thrust.

In the waterfront area, more land was reclaimed for transportation and port facilities, putting the shoreline still farther away from the city centre and making more difficult the movement of traffic from the waterfront to the downtown core. A new viaduct was built under the railways in 1930, creating seven underpasses between the Don valley and Spadina Avenue.

After 1920 the Humber and Don valleys were bridged at key points, but it was not until after the Second World War that the extension eastward of Eglinton Avenue was accomplished.

The land use map of 1941 (3-22) reveals the general form of the city at the end of the inter-war period. The residential pattern indicates a mixture of areas of various classes. In the city proper, several areas were cut by railways and were encroached upon by industrial and commercial developments. The best housing was located on ravine slopes and hilltops in both the city and the suburbs. Rooming houses were concentrated in the Don River area, around the University of Toronto

* Thomas Sharp, *Town and Countryside,* Oxford University Press, 1932

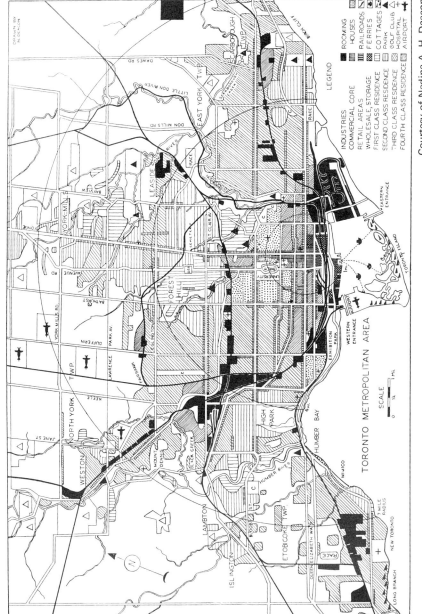

3-22: LAND USE, 1941

Courtesy of Nadine A. H. Deacon

3-23: GROWTH OF THE BUILT-UP AREA

KEY

|||||	1793-1834
■	1835-1885
░	1886-1914
▓	1915-1945
░	1946-1961

LAKE ONTARIO

0 1 2 3 4
Miles

3-24 and 3-25: The Face of Change: the Guildwood area in 1948 and in 1969

and the Parliament Buildings, and along the lakeshore to the west to accommodate visitors to the Canadian National Exhibition and other tourists.

Toronto was still a city of homeowners. In the late 1930's, it had a greater number of homeowners than Montreal, Winnipeg, and Hamilton combined. Of the 120,419 dwellings that existed in 1937, 85% of them were made of brick. This was partly a reflection of the availability of brick from companies that had located in some of the valleys, such as the Don, to use the interglacial clays that were exposed there.

In the commercial core, Yonge Street formed the principal retail strip and Bay Street the financial strip. Other retail strips had formed along main thoroughfares and contained shops of every variety. At the edges of the core, small, dingy shops did business with the lowest class residential areas. A few new suburban nuclei had also formed.

Industrial areas were concentrated along the main railway lines which followed the Humber and Don valleys, in the harbour area, and along some of the major highways. Despite the encroachment of industrial and commercial

areas, Toronto in 1941 was still a city of beautiful ravines. North of the Iroquois shore-line most of the ravines were in a natural wooded state. On the Lake Plain, the parks followed the courses of former creeks but were interrupted in many places by earlier attempts to build streets across them.

The Post-War City

In the short period that has elapsed since the end of the Second World War, Toronto has changed profoundly. There are materials in various forms in every section of this book that vividly illustrate the nature and dimensions of this change.

In 1953, recognizing the inability of some of the 12 suburban municipalities to cope with their population growth and the need for close co-operation between the municipalities and the City of Toronto, the Province of Ontario formed a new political unit—the Municipality of Metropolitan Toronto. The *municipality* is essentially a federation of local governments responsible for the administration of metro-politan services and facilities. In 1966, Metro was reorganized to form a federation of the City of Toronto and five boroughs.

SECTION 4 CITY PATTERNS

A geographical study of city patterns is essentially a study of the spatial arrangement or distribution of the various elements that, in combination, make up the total urban complex, and the ways in which these elements interact.

In the materials that follow much is revealed about the structure of Toronto. *Structure* refers to the *arrangement of the various parts of the city*—the physical patterns made by the residential, commercial, industrial and other land uses. It also refers to what some geographers call *form*—the *shapes* of the various parts and the shape of the built-up area of the city as a whole.

At the end of this section (pages 97-8) are outlines of three models of city structure. These can be used as bases for comparing the structure of Toronto with some well-established ideas of city structure in general.

4-1: SELECTED STATISTICS: AVENUE RD.—EGLINTON AVENUE AREA

CENSUS TRACT INFORMATION, 1966 CENSUS *

	Census Tract 83	Census Tract 84	Census Tract 86	Census Metropolitan Area Average
Persons Per Family, 1966	3.0	3.1	3.0	3.5
Children Per Family, 1966	1.0	1.1	1.0	1.5

ADDITIONAL DATA (FROM FIELD SURVEYS, INTERVIEWS ETC.)

Average cost of Single Family Dwelling (May 1970)	$37,500
Total School Population	330
Estimated % of Area Employees who Live in Area	40
Parking Lot Spaces	462
Metered Parking Spaces	63
Occupancy Rate, Parking Lot Spaces	30%
Occupancy Rate, Metered Parking Spaces	74%

* Source: Census of Canada, 1966. For Location of Census Tracts See Map 4-18, Page 48.

A. THE EGLINTON AVENUE-AVENUE ROAD AREA: A MICRO-STUDY

A *micro-study* is a comparatively simple yet detailed study of a small area which has been selected because in several important ways it is typical of the much larger area of which it forms a part. Because it is small its basic patterns and interactions are easy to see and explain, and since these patterns and interactions are repeated in other areas of the city and over the entire urban complex (on a much larger scale) it provides an effective basis for understanding the city as a whole.

No attempt has been made to classify the land uses shown by the various materials. The land use map (4-4) presents raw data only: a service station, for example, is shown as a service station and is not placed in any general commercial category. This allows the reader to devise any system of classification he thinks suitable for the area and to create a general land use map based on this classification:

Focal points
— The classifying of raw land use data into general categories; the creation of a general land use map
— The general patterns made by the distribution of each of the major land uses in the area
— The basic traffic patterns that an area such as this would generate, as revealed by the movement of people (on foot and in vehicles) within and through the area
— The kind of area this is today; what the area might become.

4-2: (below) The Eglinton Avenue-Avenue Road intersection, looking east along Eglinton Avenue

4-3: (right) The north side of Eglinton Avenue, looking east from Avenue Road

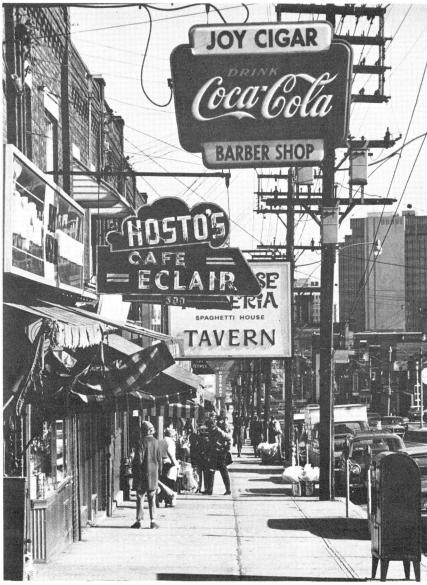

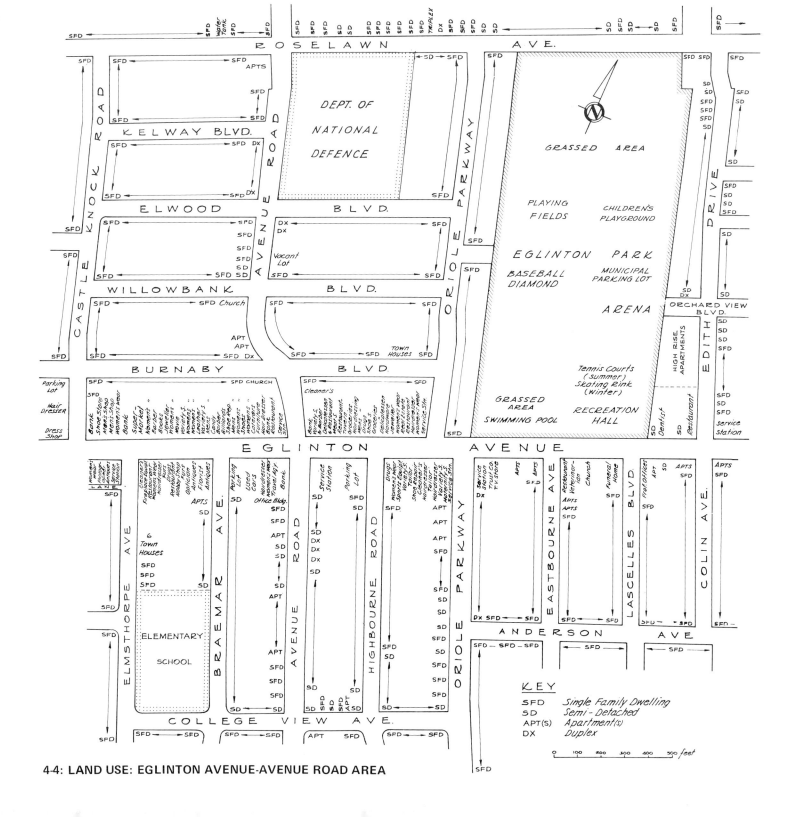

4-4: LAND USE: EGLINTON AVENUE-AVENUE ROAD AREA

4-5: The Eglinton Avenue-
Avenue Road area

39

B. PATTERNS IN THE CITY AS A WHOLE

1. COMMERCIAL LAND USE

Probably the main reason people live in cities is to do business in some form or other. In the commercial areas of a city are concentrated the many *retail, wholesale, financial,* and *service* activities that together form the principal source of employment. Moreover, these activities generate frequent interactions among people within the urban complex and make it possible for the city to dominate a large surrounding area.

Focal points
— The general pattern made by the distribution of commercial land in the city
— The proportion of the city's total area taken up by commercial land
— Differences in the form of the various commercial areas
— The location, extent, functions and appearance of the Central Business District (CBD)
— Land use patterns within the CBD
— Changes in commercial functions across the CBD
— The importance of Toronto's financial function
— The importance of the CBD in relation to other commercial areas
— Land use patterns along the edges of the CBD
— Factors influencing the value of commercial land
— Relationships between commercial areas and transportation routes
— Trends in the use of commercial land
— The patterns of Toronto's commercial districts as related to the schematic diagram (4-26) of commercial structure
— The importance of commerce to Toronto

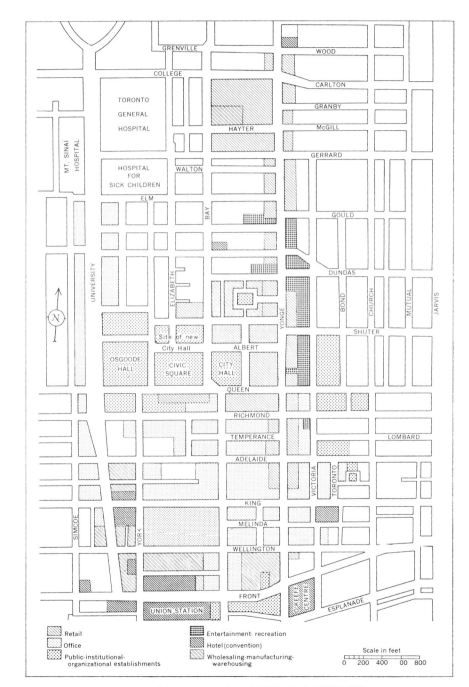

4-6: CENTRAL BUSINESS DISTRICT: GENERAL LAND USE

4-7: GROUND-LEVEL, STREET-FRONTING USES, YONGE STREET FROM FRONT STREET TO COLLEGE STREET

FRONT TO ADELAIDE

West side	East side
Dept. Store	Drug Store
ADELAIDE	**ADELAIDE**
Bank	Restaurant
Bank	Book Store
	Camera Shop
Clothing	Restaurant
Book Store	Luggage
	Restaurant
Restaurant	Jewellery
Clothing	Clothing
Restaurant	Airline Service
Jewellery	Airline Service
	Clothing
Clothing	Restaurant
	Restaurant
Clothing	Drug Store
Bank	Camera Shop
CNR Office	Bank
KING	**KING**
Bank	Bank
	CPR Passenger Service
Drug Store	Offices
	Offices
	Clothing
Jewellery	Jewellery
MELINDA	**COLBOURNE**
Office Supply	Distillers Sales
	German Airlines Service
	Custom House Brokers
Insurance	Chiropractor
	Insurance
Night Club	Carpets
	Custom House Brokers
	Jewellery
Insurance	Bank
WELLINGTON	**WELLINGTON**
Variety	
Restaurant	
Variety	
Clothing	Public
Vacant	Parking
Clothing	Lot
Restaurant	
Barber	
Parking	
Bank	
FRONT	**FRONT**
Post Office	O'Keefe Centre

(OFFICE BLDG. / OFFICE BUILDING noted along both sides between KING and WELLINGTON)

ADELAIDE TO SHUTER

West side	East side
	Tavern
	SHUTER
Shoes	Book Store
Restaurant	Furniture
Restaurant	Wine Store
Shoes	
ALBERT	Drugs
	Bank
	Tavern
	Bank
	Clothing
	Clothing
T.	Piano Sales
	Jewellery
Eaton	Theatre
	Restaurant
Dept.	Tavern
	Jewellery
Store	Optometrist
	Restaurant
	Bank
QUEEN	**QUEEN**
	Bank
	Clothing
Simpsons	Shoes
	Clothing
Dept.	Clothing
	Clothing
Store	Drug Store
	Shoes
	Clothing
	Bank
RICHMOND	**RICHMOND**
Dept.	Bank
Store	Shoes
	Restaurant
	Clothing
Restaurant	Drug Store
Clothing	Loans
	Beauty Shop
Gifts	Shopping Mall
TEMPERANCE	Camera Shop
Jewellery	Shoe Clinic
	Restaurant
	Clothing
Shoes	Shoe Repair
Shoes	Shoes
	Office Supply
Dept.	Loans
Store	Drug Store
ADELAIDE	**ADELAIDE**
Bank	Restaurant

SHUTER TO GOULD

West side	East side
Funland	Bank
Appliances	**GOULD**
Restaurant	Tavern
Furs	Tavern
Clothing	Book Store
Billiards	Clothing
Sewing Centre	Clothing
Furniture	Jewellery
EDWARD	Restaurant
	Theatre
Parking	Restaurant
	Cleaners
Music Store	Restaurant
Bank	Tavern
DUNDAS	**DUNDAS**
Clothing	Clothing
Optical Shop	
Camera Shop	Book Store
Clothing	
Book Store	Drug Store
Shoes	
Optometrist	Furniture
Clothing	
Clothing	
Camera Shop	Theatre
Shoes	
TERAULAY	**DUNDAS SQ.**
Tie Shop	Tavern
Shoes	Book Store
Camera Shop	Jewellery
Jewellery	Clothing
Clothing	Jewellery
Shoes	Clothing
Camera Shop	Restaurant
Shoes	Clothing
Hat Shop	Theatre
Shoes	Jewellery
Shoes	Restaurant
Shoes	Restaurant
TRINITY SQ.	Clothing
Radio-TV Sales	Restaurant
Textiles	Shoes
Sewing Centre	Supper Club
Clothing	Wig Mart
Record Shop	Shoes
Clothing	Shoes
Shoes	Sporting Goods
Furs	Luggage
LOUISA	Shoes
Furniture	Clothing
TV Rentals	Clothing
Shoes	Drug Store
Clothing	Tavern
Clothing	**SHUTER**
	Book Store

GOULD TO COLLEGE

West side	East side
Bank	Candy Shop
COLLEGE	**CARLTON**
	Department Store
	Photography
T. Eaton College St. Department Store	Travel Agency
	Sporting Goods
	Restaurant
	Drug Store
	GRANBY
Stores for Lease	Senior Citizen Apartments under Construction
HAYTER	**McGILL**
Hair Salon	Parking Lot
Cleaners	
Clothing	Barber
Restaurant	Barber
Food Store	Restaurant
Restaurant	Clothing
Gifts	Theatre
GERRARD	**GERRARD**
Bank	Restaurant
Jewellery	CBC TV Prods. Offices
Gift Shop	Mission
Hosiery	Tavern
Restaurant	Clothing
WALTON	Theatre
Wig Shop	Clothing
Clothing	Book Store
Photographer	Restaurant
Barber	Luggage
Furs	Clothing
Restaurant	Tie Shop
Billiards	Clothing
Furniture	Tavern
Clothing	Drug Store
Barber	Restaurant
Restaurant	Optometrist
Watch Shop	Book Store
Optometrist	Jewellery
Flowers	Record Shop
ELM	Tavern
Restaurant	Record Shop
Camera Shop	Clothing
China Shop	Bank
Clothing	**GOULD**
	Tavern

Data obtained by field survey November 1969

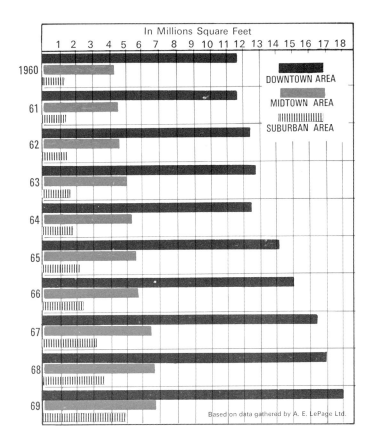

In Millions Square Feet

	1 2 3 4 5 6 7 8 9 10 11 12 13 14 15 16 17 18
1960	
61	
62	
63	
64	
65	
66	
67	
68	
69	

DOWNTOWN AREA

MIDTOWN AREA

SUBURBAN AREA

Based on data gathered by A. E. LePage Ltd.

4-9: METROPOLITAN TORONTO: GROWTH IN SUPPLY OF OFFICE SPACE, 1960-69 ACTUAL

SUBURBAN

mid town

down town

UNIVERSITY AVENUE   YONGE STREET

4-10: The Central Business District

THE FREDERICK G. GARDINER EXPRESSWAY

FRONT STREET

KING STREET

QUEEN STREET

JARVIS STREET

YONGE STREET

UNIVERSITY AVENUE

COLLEGE STREET

4-11: The Central Business District. South is toward the top of the photo

4-12: The western edge of the CBD

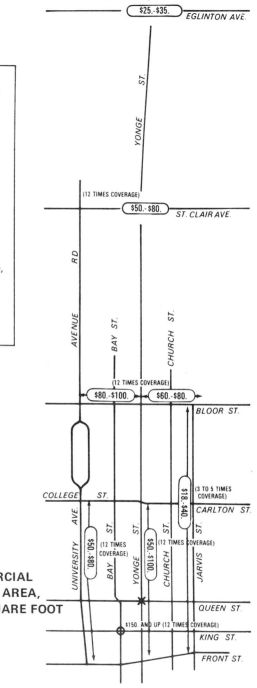

4-13: The eastern edge of the CBD from the top of the Toronto Dominion Tower, looking east

4-14: SELECTED CENSUS TRACT INFORMATION*
(1966 CENSUS)

	Census Tract 60 (W. Side of CBD)	Census Tract 99 (E. Side of CBD)	Census Tract 1 (Resid. Area 4½ Mi. W. of CBD)	Census Tract 84 (Resid. Area 3½ Mi. N. of CBD)
Population 1966	4,833	6,005	7,712	4,877
Population 1961	4,919	6,163	8,050	5,031
Occupied Dwellings (Households**)	951	1,270	2,204	1,687
Owner-Occupied Dwellings	359	320	1,567	917
Tenant-Occupied Dwellings	592	950	637	770
Single Attached Dwellings	439	489	286	397
Single Detached Dwellings	138	157	1,281	636
Apartments, Flats	374	624	637	654
Persons per Household	4.4	3.3	3.5	2.9
Persons per Family	3.5	3.3	3.1	3.1
Children per Family	1.6	1.3	1.1	1.1

*For Location of Census Tracts Refer to Map 4-18, Page 48.

**A Household Consists of a Person or Group of Persons Occupying One Dwelling.

The value of land is the result of the combined effect of many factors and is constantly changing. The prime factor, of course, is the use to which the land can be put. Zoning laws, for example, exert a very strong influence. In some areas, such as the downtown area, the City allows the total area of floor space of a building to be 12 times as much as the total area of the property on which the building is constructed. In other areas only 5 times as much is allowed; in others still, only 3 times as much. Also, the supply of and demand for property at any particular time can change rapidly and drive values up or down. Therefore, the commercial land value ranges indicated on Map 4-15 give a very general picture only and are not to be regarded as definitive for any particular area or property.

4-15: ESTIMATED COMMERCIAL LAND VALUES: CENTRAL AREA, SPRING 1970 IN $ PER SQUARE FOOT

X Peak Land Value Intersection in 1965
O 1970 Peak Land Value Intersection:
$150. per sq. ft. and up
Based on data gathered by A. E. LePage Ltd.

45

4-16: Outlying business centres, looking north along Yonge Street. Foreground: the Yonge Street-St. Clair Avenue centre; background (last row of tall buildings): the Yonge Street-Eglinton Avenue centre

Census Tract	Total All Stores No. of Stores	Total All Stores Sales $ '000	Food Group No. of Stores	Food Group Sales $ '000	General Merchandise Group No. of Stores	General Merchandise Group Sales $ '000
47	97	6,336	41	2,249	2	— —
61	84	4,827	25	1,228	1	— —
62	63	4,093	15	1,002	1	— —
73*	158	177,858	23	2,586	7	140,065
74*	140	60,050	9	— —	2	— —
101	48	5,577	20	3,185	—	—
304	27	5,920	10	816	—	—

Census Tract	Total All Stores No. of Stores	Total All Stores Sales $ '000	Food Group No. of Stores	Food Group Sales $ '000	General Merchandise Group No. of Stores	General Merchandise Group Sales $ '000
67	18	6,566	2	— —	—	—
68	15	1,256	3	573	—	—
69	40	3,816	9	1,169	—	—
70	167	32,979	12	— —	2	— —
71	203	49,269	17	— —	1	— —
73*	158	177,858	23	2,586	7	140,065
75	134	128,774	7	— —	3	103,444

*Census Tracts 73 and 74 lie within the CBD.

STATISTICS OF RETAIL TRADE   STATISTICS OF SERVICE TRADES

** CENSUS TRACTS ALONG QUEEN STREET (E—W)

Automotive Group		Apparel & Accessories Group		Hardware & Home Furnishing Group		Other Retail Stores Group		Total, All Locations		Amusement and Recreation Group		Business Services Group		Personal Services Group		Repair Services Group		Hotel, Tourist, Camp and Restaurant Group		Miscellaneous Services Group	
No. of Stores	Sales $'000	No. of Stores	Sales $'000	No. of Stores	Sales $'000	No. of Stores	Sales $'000	No. of Locations	Receipts $'000	No. of Locations	Receipts $'000	No. of Locations	Receipts $'000	No. of Locations	Receipts $'000	No. of Locations	Receipts $'000	No. of Locations	Receipts $'000	No. of Locations	Receipts $'000
2	— —	24	1,028	7	456	21	2,244	41	1,009	3	82	—	—	23	232	—	—	12	651	3	45
3	— —	31	1,777	9	414	15	844	38	6,206	3	43	2	— —	17	5,300	1	— —	14	838	1	— —
5	626	12	— —	10	623	20	1,054	67	8,484	4	848	3	69	29	1,178	—	—	25	1,934	6	4,455
9	20,347	49	6,142	18	3,333	52	5,386	138	17,537	11	1,196	13	3,934	36	768	—	—	68	10,594	10	1,046
1	11,097	28	6,651	8	3,209	82	15,317	156	35,537	26	16,593	12	— —	44	1,092	2	— —	63	13,085	9	3,396
5	1,244	8	382	10	388	5	378	32	1,062	1	— —	1	— —	17	629	—	—	12	398	1	— —
4	555	5	80	3	294	5	4,176	21	708	2	— —	—	—	6	59	—	—	12	433	1	— —

Key
— —   Figures Not Available
—   Nil or Zero

CENSUS TRACTS ALONG YONGE STREET (N—S)

Automotive Group		Apparel & Accessories Group		Hardware & Home Furnishing Group		Other Retail Stores Group		Total, All Locations		Amusement and Recreation Group		Business Services Group		Personal Services Group		Repair Services Group		Hotel, Tourist, Camp and Restaurant Group		Miscellaneous Services Group	
No. of Stores	Sales $'000	No. of Stores	Sales $'000	No. of Stores	Sales $'000	No. of Stores	Sales $'000	No. of Locations	Receipts $'000	No. of Locations	Receipts $'000	No. of Locations	Receipts $'000	No. of Locations	Receipts $'000	No. of Locations	Receipts $'000	No. of Locations	Receipts $'000	No. of Locations	Receipts $'000
1	— —	7	501	3	622	5	882	24	1,990	2	— —	4	96	12	283	—	—	5	1,070	1	— —
3	— —	1	— —	5	94	3	341	16	3,236	1	— —	2	— —	10	128	—	—	3	132	—	—
3	940	4	143	12	668	12	897	43	6,488	4	1,715	9	2,463	18	373	—	—	9	461	3	1,477
3	12,037	56	9,313	27	3,363	57	4,291	162	21,753	18	5,014	54	10,123	35	1,859	—	—	41	4,246	14	511
9	27,156	72	9,451	20	3,559	84	7,948	149	44,575	14	6,493	25	11,072	47	— —	2	— —	50	6,494	11	18,539
9	20,347	49	6,142	18	3,333	52	5,386	138	17,537	11	1,196	13	3,934	36	768	—	—	68	10,594	10	1,046
1	— —	36	6,341	6	2,011	81	16,311	392	93,925	24	7,182	209	50,699	47	— —	1	— —	86	30,134	25	4,520

**For location of census tracts used in this table refer to Map 4-18, page 48.   Source: 1966 Census of Canada

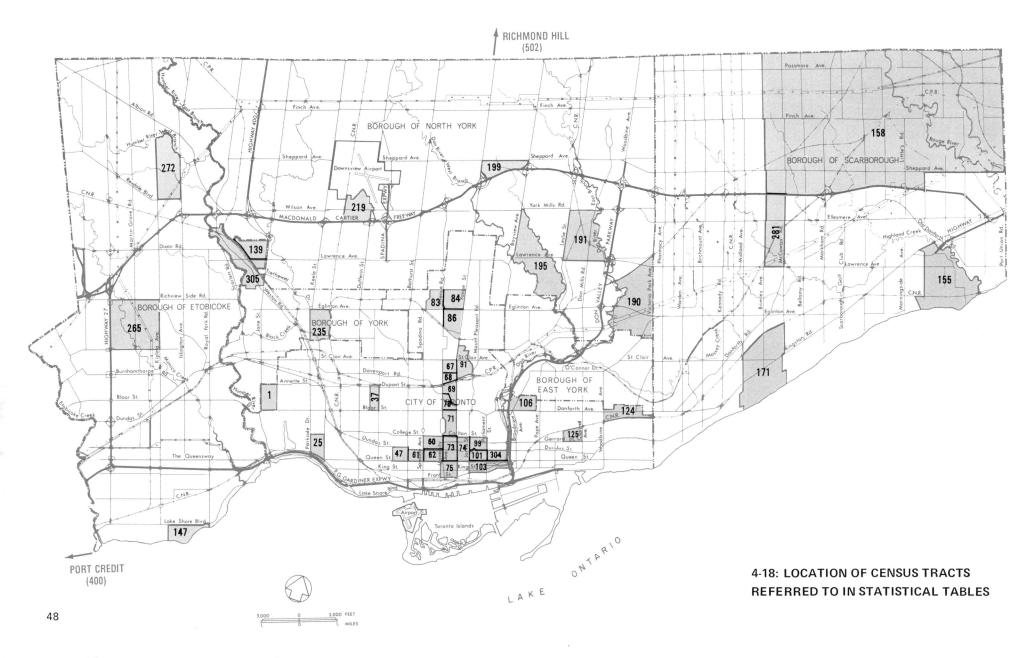

4-18: LOCATION OF CENSUS TRACTS REFERRED TO IN STATISTICAL TABLES

4-19, 4-20, 4-21: College Street at Clinton
Avenue, 1½ miles west of Yonge Street: a
neighbourhood business district

4-22: *Yorkdale Plaza: a controlled regional shopping centre. South is toward the top of the photo.*

4-23: LABOUR FORCE IN FINANCE AND CHEQUES CASHED AT CLEARING HOUSES FOR SELECTED CENSUS METROPOLITAN AREAS (OVER 100,000) IN 1961

Census Metropolitan Area	Labour Force in Finance	Ratio of Labour Force in Finance to Total Labour Force	Labour Force in Investment Companies and Security Dealers	Cheques Cashed * $000,000
Calgary	5,566	5.0	445	10,300
Edmonton	5,467	4.1	328	6,700
Halifax	2,988	4.1	137	2,800
Hamilton	4,969	3.3	213	6,000
Kitchener-Waterloo	3,152	4.8	—	1,300
London	4,580	6.2	163	3,700
Montreal	41,984	5.2	3,649	78,600
Ottawa	7,480	4.4	205	5,900
Quebec (City)	5,127	4.0	211	7,900
Regina	2,530	5.4	113	4,900
Sudbury	994	2.5	—	700
Toronto	52,338	6.6	5,703	109,600
Vancouver	15,918	5.4	1,165	17,800
Victoria	2,244	4.0	143	2,700
Windsor	2,690	3.9	155	2,400
Winnipeg	10,252	5.3	830	20,900
Total for Canada	**228,905**	**3.5**	**15,459**	**293,784**

*Source: D.B.S., Canada Year Book 1962 (Ottawa, 1962), p. 1105
Source: Census of Canada 1961, vol. 3.

— Less than 100

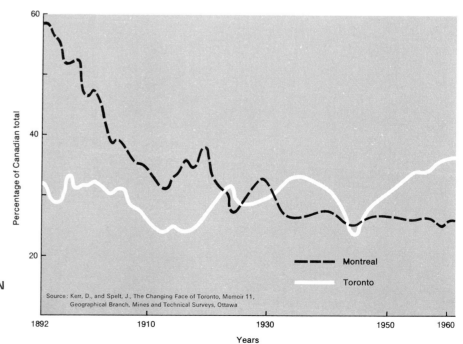

4-24: BANK CLEARINGS AS A PERCENTAGE OF THE CANADIAN TOTAL, TORONTO AND MONTREAL, 1892-1961

Source: Kerr, D., and Spelt, J., The Changing Face of Toronto, Memoir 11, Geographical Branch, Mines and Technical Surveys, Ottawa

4-25: RETAIL TRADE AND SERVICE TRADES—TORONTO CENSUS METROPOLITAN AREA —1966

RETAIL TRADE

Total All Stores		Food Group		General Merchandise Group		Automotive Group		Apparel and Accessories Group		Hardware and Home Furnishings Group		Other Retail Stores Group	
No. of Stores	Sales $ '000	No. of Stores	Sales $ '000	No. of Stores	Sales $ '000	No. of Stores	Sales $ '000	No. of Stores	Sales $ '000	No. of Stores	Sales $ '000	No. of Stores	Sales $ '000
14,183	2,989,273	3,603	767,598	276	489,815	2,471	833,717	2,627	214,013	1,751	202,768	3,455	481,362

SERVICE TRADES

Total All Locations		Amusement and Recreation Group		Business Services Group		Personal Services Group		Repair Services Group		Hotel, Tourist, Camp and Restaurant Group		Miscellaneous Services Group	
No. of Loc.	Receipts $ '000	No. of Loc.	Receipts $ '000	No. of Loc.	Receipts $ '000	No. of Loc.	Receipts $ '000	No. of Loc.	Receipts $ '000	No. of Loc.	Receipts $ '000	No. of Loc.	Receipts $ '000
10,297	850,117	690	114,292	1,246	192,199	4,791	112,391	160	6,718	2,729	290,602	681	133,916

Source: 1966 Census of Canada

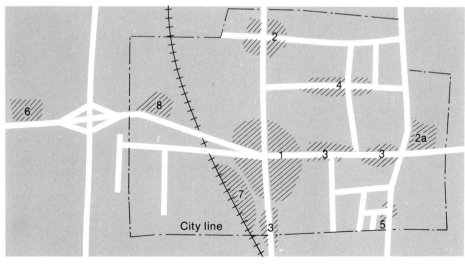

4-26: COMMERCIAL STRUCTURE OF A CITY

Map 4-26 is a schematic diagram showing the types of commercial areas that usually develop in a city.

Key
1. Central Business District
2. Outlying Business Centre
2a. Controlled Outlying Business Centre
3. Principal Business Thoroughfare
4. Neighbourhood Business Street
5. Isolated Store Cluster
6. Controlled Regional Shopping Centre
7. Railroad-oriented Wholesale Area
8. Highway-oriented Wholesale Development

Source: *The American City*, by Raymond E. Murphy. © 1966 by McGraw-Hill, Inc. Used with permission of McGraw-Hill Book Company

2. INDUSTRIAL LAND USE

The term *industry,* as it is used in this section, means *manufacturing*—the changing of the form of certain materials for the purpose of rendering them more useful and increasing their value.

Not all manufacturing, of course, is carried on in cities. So much of it is located in or around the edges of them, however, that it forms an important area of study for the urban geographer.

Focal points

— The general pattern made by the distribution of industrial land in the city
— The proportion of the city's total area taken up by industrial land
— The diversity of manufacturing in Toronto
— The most important manufacturing industries in Toronto
— Contrasts and trends in
     the appearance, size, and types of manu-
     facturing plants
     the density of manufacturing plants
     industrial employment
     value of shipments of manufactured
     goods in Toronto
— The impact of industrial areas on adjacent areas
— General and particular factors affecting the location of manufacturing industries in Toronto
— The patterns of Toronto's manufacturing districts as related to the schematic diagram (4-39) of manufacturing districts
— The drawing power of Toronto as a location for industries
— The proportion of goods manufactured in Toronto that are consumed in Toronto
— The importance of manufacturing to Toronto

4-27: MANUFACTURING INDUSTRIES
PRINCIPAL STATISTICS—ALL-INDUSTRY TOTALS 1964

	Establishments	Production and Related Workers		Value Added By Manufacturing Activities $'000	Total Employees	Value of Shipments of Goods of Own Manufacture $'000
		Male	Female			
City of Toronto	2,600	50,966	25,467	954,639	108,068	2,150,420
Borough of North York	676	19,151	7,099	357,194	40,160	689,219
Borough of Scarborough	445	10,925	3,108	190,949	20,666	374,591
Borough of Etobicoke	648	19,397	5,440	389,218	36,650	804,208
Borough of York	295	7,061	2,335	135,196	14,224	271,749
Borough of East York	149	6,233	3,570	117,341	15,429	262,299
Metropolitan Toronto	4,813	113,733	47,019	2,144,537	235,197	4,552,486
Toronto Census Metropolitan Area	5,352	131,311	50,027	2,511,092	263,325	5,657,516
Province of Ontario	12,781	402,373	107,385	7,066,985	728,936	15,842,949
Canada	33,630	1,057,502 (Total)		13,535,991	1,491,257	30,856,099
Montreal C.M.A.	5,398	121,094	61,852	2,163,835	253,919	4,866,656
Vancouver C.M.A.	1,838	35,265	6,637	538,581	57,375	1,294,328
Winnipeg C.M.A.	1,028	18,427	7,506	280,865	35,787	727,130
Calgary C.M.A.	439	6,256	976	117,019	11,103	337,460

Source: D.B.S.—Manufacturing Industries of Canada, 1964

4-28 TORONTO CENSUS METROPOLITAN AREA INDUSTRIES, 1964

Industry	Establish- ments No.	Employees No.	Value of Shipments of Goods of Own Manufacture $'000	Industry	Establish- ments No.	Employees No.	Value of Shipments of Goods of Own Manufacture $'000
Aluminum Rolling, Casting and Extruding	12	862	16,457,000	Metal Roll Cast, Extruded	23	1,281	55,169,000
Artificial Flowers and Feathers	10	43	409,000	Metal Stamp and Press Etc.	173	7,518	150,484,000
Bakeries	240	6,130	87,257,000	Models and Patterns	29	443	6,807,000
Biscuits	7	1,507	29,648,000	Motor Vehicle Parts	42	3,901	74,640,000
Boatbuilding and Repair	13	137	1,701,000	Musical Instruments and Sound Recording	9	526	7,911,000
Boiler and Plate Works	12	618	9,126,000	Narrow Fabrics	8	149	1,654,000
Boxes, Corrugated	13	1,694	40,260,000	Ophthalmic Goods	8	708	6,166,000
Boxes, Folding and Set Up	34	2,891	50,623,000	Orthopaedic, Surgical Appl.	12	203	2,548,000
Breweries	5	1,258	71,096,000	Other Misc. Industries	39	1,191	14,746,000
Brooms, Brushes and Mops	8	339	3,715,000	Paints and Varnishes	45	2,814	80,619,000
Canvas Products	24	467	6,020,000	Paper Converters Misc.	73	5,728	98,537,000
Chemicals, Industrial	16	921	24,608,000	Pharmaceutical and Medicine	49	3,572	64,989,000
Chemical Industries, Other	119	3,542	93,806,000	Plastic Fabricators	122	3,599	56,376,000
Clay Products, Domestic	8	861	13,515,000	Plastic Synthetic Resin	8	325	16,170,000
Clocks and Watches	11	533	13,094,000	Poultry Processors	6	135	6,388,000
Clothing, Children	31	1,427	12,469,000	Printing, Commercial	463	12,183	174,863,000
Clothing, Contractor Men	13	182	921,000	Printing and Publishing	46	7,728	118,081,000
Clothing, Contractor Women	15	420	1,606,000	Publishing Only	136	1,657	29,435,000
Clothing, Men's Factory	94	6,208	59,664,000	Pulp and Paper	5	762	25,991,000
Clothing, Women's Factory	145	5,618	65,081,000	Radio, Television Receiver	8	3,158	63,235,000
Communications Equipment	54	6,800	90,459,000	Refrigeration and Air Cond., Commercial	6	211	3,041,000
Concrete Products	57	2,282	34,397,000	Sash, Door, Planing Mills	84	1,867	29,982,000
Concrete, Ready Mix	18	1,056	39,900,000	Sausage, Sausage Casing	17	428	11,583,000
Confectionery	36	4,032	79,125,000	Shoe Factories	40	1,873	19,124,000
Cotton and Jute Bags	6	148	4,141,000	Signs and Displays	102	2,044	24,004,000
Dairy Factories	42	3,002	76,235,000	Soap Cleaning Compounds	34	2,825	93,116,000
Dental Laboratories	60	485	4,619,000	Soft Drinks	24	1,747	32,371,000
Distilleries	4	394	17,480,000	Sporting Goods	26	1,692	25,182,000
Electric Appliances, Major	11	3,659	78,678,000	Stamps, Stencils, Rubber Merc.	20.	348	2,746,000
Electric Appliances, Small	28	2,056	44,342,000	Statuary Art Goods, Etc.	29	338	3,368,000
Electric Industrial Equipment	42	6,430	105,501,000	Stone Products	16	190	3,075,000
Embroideries, Pleating, Etc.	28	428	2,828,000	Textile Dyeing, Finishing	15	320	3,670,000
Engraving and Duplicating Plates	106	2,657	29,442,000	Toilet Preparations	29	1,880	42,986,000
Feeds	22	709	30,052,000	Toys and Games	40	2,147	25,994,000
Fibre, Preparing	9	224	4,818,000	Truck Body and Trailers	16	1,274	26,159,000
Foundation Garments	6	1,227	13,952,000	Typewriters Supplies	5	446	7,441,000
Fountain Pens and Pencils	6	386	6,660,000	Venetian Blinds	8	45	514,000
Fur Goods	110	749	15,012,000	Wire and Wire Products	64	2,543	49,189,000
Furniture, Household	296	4,164	63,250,000	Wooden boxes	10	296	3,526,000
Furniture, Office	12	567	7,562,000	All Other Clothing Industries	14	377	3,928,000
Glass and Glass Products	36	1,936	32,737,000	All Other Electrical Products	78	7,829	171,557,000
Hardware, Tools, Cutlery	118	3,202	45,811,000	All Other Food and Beverages	146	11,296	580,261,000
Hats and Caps	32	571	4,428,000	All Other Furniture Industries	105	2,887	45,834,000
Heating Equipment	32	1,532	29,042,000	All Other Leather Products	59	2,096	24,107,000
Hosiery Mills	19	933	11,014,000	All Other Machinery	17	6,852	149,488,000
Instruments and Related	47	4,895	84,259,000	All Other Non-Metallic Industries	21	1,634	44,015,000
Iron Foundries	7	716	14,764,000	All Other Paper and Allied Industries	17	1,162	27,125,000
Jewellery and Silverware	104	2,564	45,890,000	All Other Primary Metal Industries	17	1,779	64,087,000
Knitting Mills, Other	42	2,297	26,647,000	All Other Textile Industries	106	4,999	83,332,000
Lamp, Electric, Lamp Shades	23	478	6,011,000	All Other Transportation Equipment Ind.	22	16,744	618,160,000
Machine Shops	140	1,580	17,549,000	All Other Wood Industries	27	800	8,941,000
Machinery Misc.	146	8,091	139,749,000	All Other Industries	38	6,950	340,774,000
Metal Fabricating, Misc.	116	4,537	82,349,000				
Metal Fabricating, Structural	16	3,613	80,005,000	**TOTAL**	**5,352**	**263,325**	**$5,657,516,000**
Metal, Ornament, Architect	135	3,767	64,245,000				

Source: Metropolitan Toronto Industrial Commission

4-29, 4-30: Part of the garment district along lower Spadina Avenue: an older light manufacturing district. Looking south, coloured area on Photo 4-30 shows the location of the buildings illustrated in Photo 4-29.

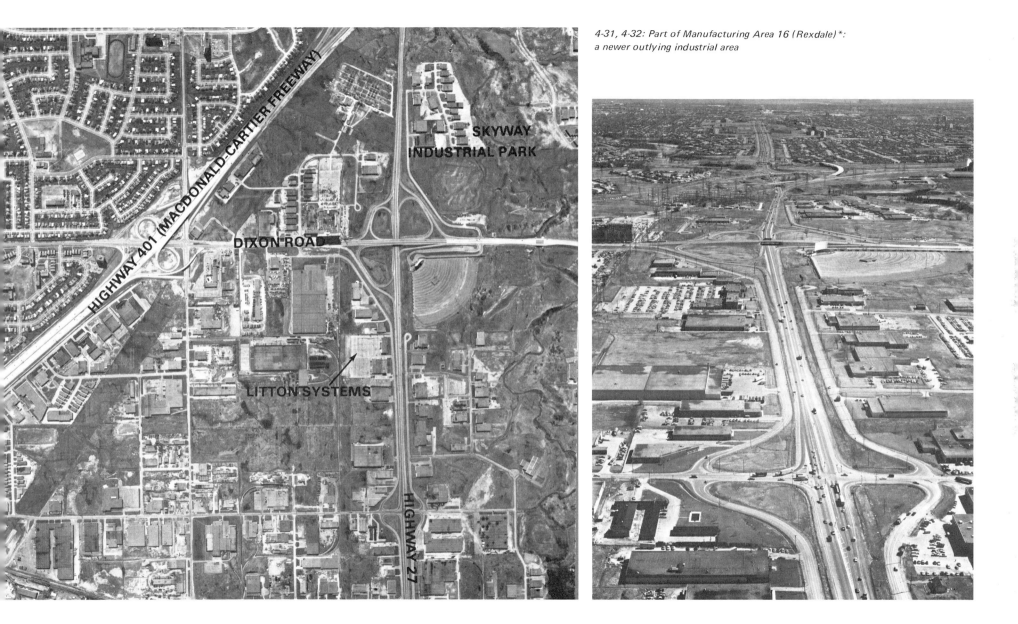

SKYWAY INDUSTRIAL PARK

HIGHWAY 401 (MACDONALD-CARTIER FREEWAY)

DIXON ROAD

LITTON SYSTEMS

HIGHWAY 27

4-31, 4-32: Part of Manufacturing Area 16 (Rexdale)*:
a newer outlying industrial area

*See Map 4-33, page 56

55

KEY

	Area	Employment
1.	Downtown	30,811
2.	Parkdale	13,361
3.	Don	6,734
4.	Harbour	8,542
5.	Junction	21,226
6.	Dupont	4,211
7.	Greenwood	5,244
8.	Lakeshore	7,797
9.	Leaside	6,509
10.	East York	7,957
11.	Oak Ridge	5,602
12.	Scarborough	11,348
13.	Don Mills	11,026
14.	Weston	5,559
15.	York	13,240
16.	Rexdale	7,634
17.	North York	5,499
18.	S. Etobicoke	18,573

3,750
3,000
2,250
1,500
750

} Number of employees in manufacturing

Food
Textiles
Wood
Metal
Machinery
Chemical

0 1 2 3 4 5

Miles

LAKE ONTARIO

4-33: MANUFACTURING AREAS IN METROPOLITAN TORONTO, 1964

56

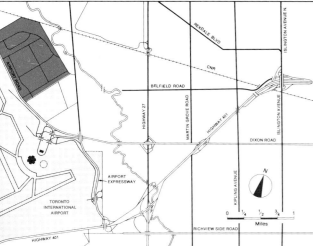

4-34: A part of Airport Industrial Park

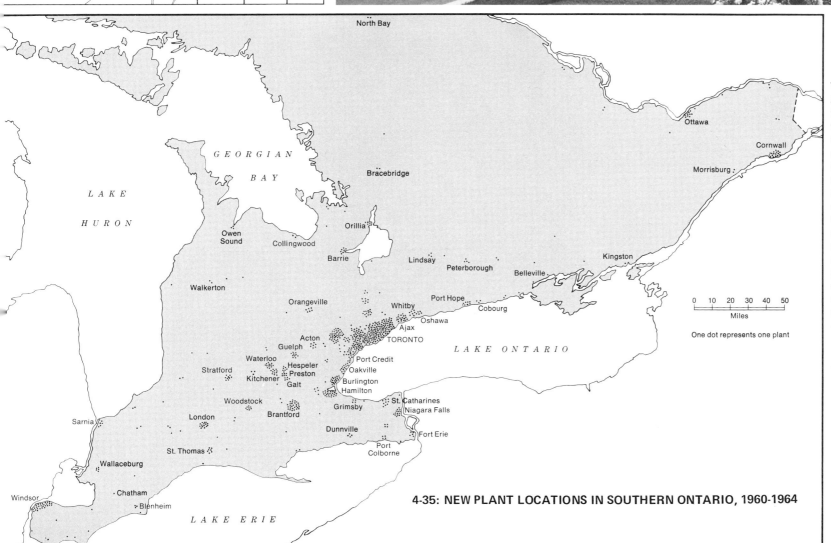

4-35: NEW PLANT LOCATIONS IN SOUTHERN ONTARIO, 1960-1964

One dot represents one plant

0 10 20 30 40 50
Miles

The Industrial Park

A recent development in the field of industrial location is the *industrial park*. While there is no general agreement about precisely what an industrial park is, the term is widely used today to refer to a general kind of industrial area that is different enough from other kinds to be fairly distinctive. Industrial parks are often areas developed by and under the control of one property owner. Many are attractively landscaped, self-contained areas which provide a wide range of services such as road, water, sewerage and power systems, and which may contain buildings that are available for rent but not for sale. Others may consist of a group of adjacent properties for which there is no fully integrated system of services. Some contain buildings that are actually sold to the various industrial companies concerned. Usually, an industrial park is located along the fringe of an urban area.

Litton Systems (Canada) Limited, Litton Industries, 25 Cityview Drive, Rexdale, Ontario, Canada

Production: "Airborne Avionics"
aviation and electronic equipment associated with inertial navigation

Historical Background
Litton Systems is basically a manufacturing arm of the U.S. sales division of Litton Industries Inc., Beverly Hills, California.

Litton founded its Canadian subsidiary in 1960 to manufacture the guidance system it had developed for a U.S. jet fighter, the F-104 (Lockheed Aircraft).

Servo Mechanisims was a small company operating in the military electronics/electro-mechanical field at 123 Rexdale Blvd. This company became the nucleus from which Litton Systems grew, following a takeover in the late 1950's.

Locational Factors
available technology (skills) in the area (34 skilled technicians came to Litton from Servo; 12 remain with the firm today)

proximity to the Toronto International Airport

proximity to Customs

a stipulation in the Canadian contract to purchase the F-104 from Lockheed Aircraft, that Lockheed and its subcontractors—in this case Litton—would undertake to produce a large percentage of the aircraft in Canada

Montreal firms were under full production and employment—AVRO in Toronto had just lost a government contract to produce the Arrow jet fighter (1957).

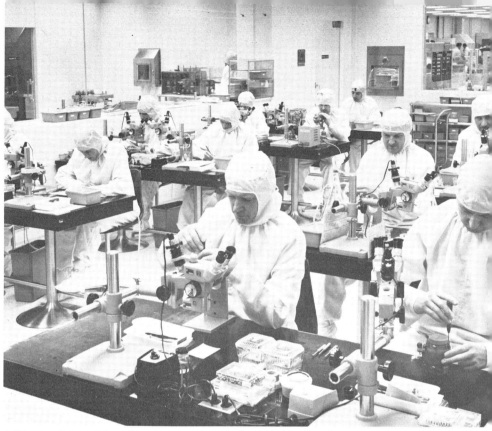

4-37: Since "state of the art" components in today's sophisticated equipment are measured in millionths of an inch, they must be assembled in dust-free, humidity- and temperature-controlled areas such as Litton Systems' 4,000 square-foot Super Clean Room. All environmental control equipment is completely duplicated to ensure continuous operation.

4-36

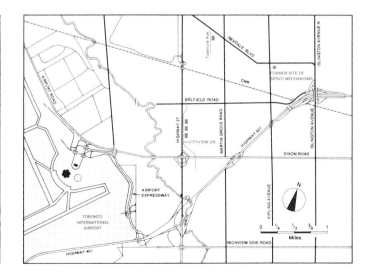

4-38: RESULTS OF TRANSPORTATION COST STUDIES

Studies based on data supplied by manufacturers are frequently made by the Metropolitan Toronto Industrial Commission to help them decide on their most economical location. The following are the results which show the annual savings in transportation costs by having a plant at Toronto over other possible communities under comparison:

Finished Product	Distance from Toronto to Community under Comparison	Savings at Toronto per truckload or carload*	Total Annual Savings at Toronto†	Annual Savings related to cost at Toronto
Air-conditioners	57 miles	$127	$ 55,539	14%
Air-conditioners	160	139	60,897	15
Automobiles	349	117	328,000	37
Automobiles	519	153	431,400	49
Beer	190	51	255,475	44
Building Materials	35	14	15,564	9
Cereals	35	147	7,085	115
Chemicals	90	92	6,573	38
Chemicals	250	267	19,122	109
Greeting Cards	98	650	129,495	46
Lift Trucks	140	262	38,682	187
Office Equipment	35	90	10,470	12
Office Equipment	105	275	32,080	36
Stationery	70	75	9,648	33
Tires	82	312	71,181	86
Toys	68	221	7,365	31
Vegetable Oil	90	21	82,401	25

* Assumed to be 30,000 lbs.

† Total dollar savings depend upon the weight shipped annually and patterns of distribution.

Source: Metropolitan Toronto Industrial Commission

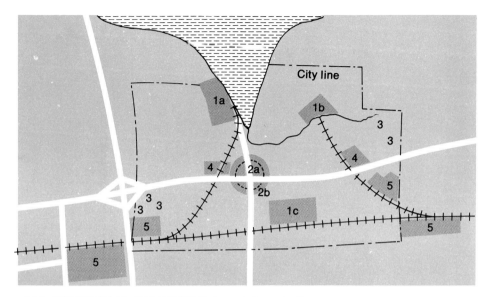

4-39: INDUSTRIAL STRUCTURE OF A MIDDLE-SIZED MANUFACTURING CITY

Map 4-39 is a schematic diagram showing the various types of manufacturing areas that usually develop in a typical middle-sized city.

Key
1a. Manufacturing Area on Waterfront
1b. Manufacturing Area at Waterfall
1c. Manufacturing Area along Railroad
2a. Light Manufacturing Area Serving Central Business District
2b. Area of Loft-Type Factories
3. Scattered Factories in Residential Areas
4. Manufacturing Area Resulting from Clearance and Redevelopment
5. Outlying Manufacturing Area

Source: *The American City,* by Raymond E. Murphy. © 1966 by McGraw-Hill, Inc. Used with permission of McGraw-Hill Book Company

3. POPULATION AND LABOUR FORCE*

The word *city* suggests many things: tall buildings, traffic jams, pollution, shops, factories and above all, a multitude of people. To state the obvious, a city is people more than it is anything else. It is man's creation and in many parts of the world his principal home.

Urban geographers are giving increased attention today to the spatial aspects of city population. Studies of this kind can lead to important understandings of the city's social and economic character.

This section is included with the set of land use studies because, even though people themselves do not constitute a land use as such, many of their characteristics can be shown in the form of spatial patterns, as an examination of the materials that follow will indicate.

Focal points
— The patterns of population distribution and density in Toronto; the relationships of these patterns to other land use patterns
— The age and sex characteristics of the population; gradients (differences) in age and sex structure across the city
— Relationships between
    income and population patterns
    labour force and population patterns
    income and labour force patterns
— The ethnic composition of Toronto and factors affecting the distribution of ethnic groups
— Trends in population growth in Toronto
— Toronto's functions as revealed by labour force data
— The impact of population and labour force characteristics on the city's landscape

---

* The Dominion Bureau of Statistics defines *labour force* as those people, 14 years of age and over, who are either employed or looking for work.

4-40: POPULATION GROWTH OF THE CITY OF TORONTO, METROPOLITAN TORONTO, THE METROPOLITAN TORONTO PLANNING AREA, THE PROVINCE OF ONTARIO, AND CANADA FOR SELECTED CENSUS YEARS 1861-1966*

	1861	1881	1901	1921	1941	1956	1966
Canada	3,229,633	4,324,810	5,371,315	8,787,949	11,506,655	16,080,791	20,014,880
Ontario	1,396,091	1,926,922	2,182,947	2,933,662	3,787,655	5,404,933	6,960,870
M.T.P.A.	98,750	143,892	263,454	640,002	950,490	1,475,811	2,100,370
Met. Tor.	65,085	113,128	238,080	611,443	909,928	1,358,028	1,881,691
City of Tor.	44,821	86,415	208,040	521,893	667,457	667,706	664,584

*Population figures for the places listed relate to the boundaries of those places as they existed at the respective census dates. Many boundary changes occurred, of course, during the period 1861-1966.

Sources: — Census of Canada
        — Metropolitan Toronto Planning Board

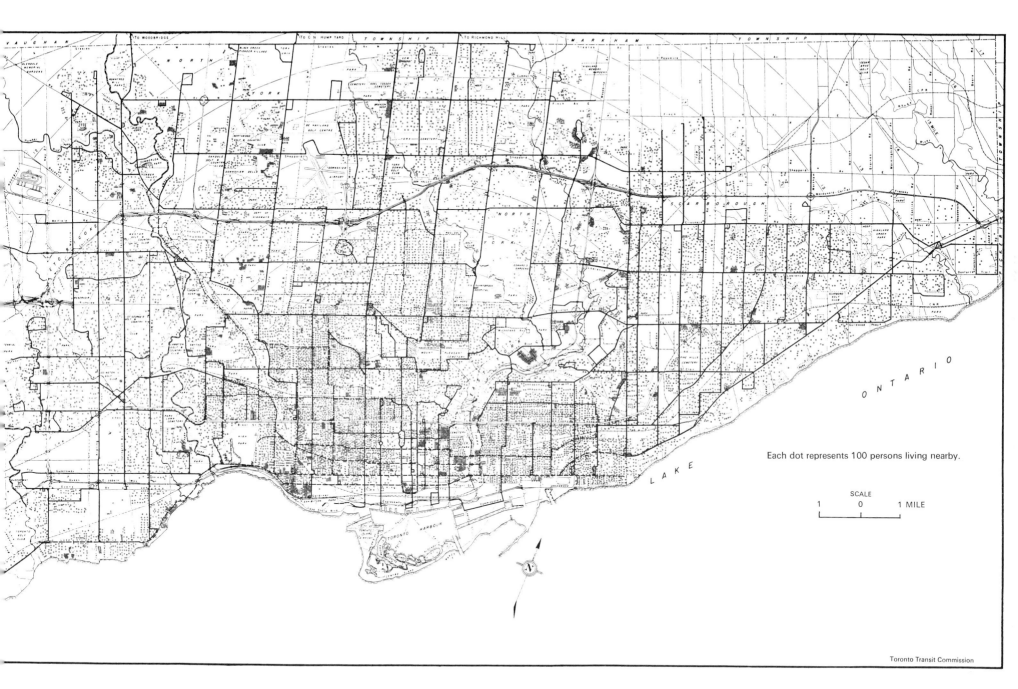

Each dot represents 100 persons living nearby.

SCALE

1   0   1 MILE

Toronto Transit Commission

4-41: POPULATION DISTRIBUTION IN METROPOLITAN TORONTO, 1968

4-42: POPULATION, FIVE-YEAR GROWTH RATES, CANADIAN METROPOLITAN AREAS 1951-1966

Census Metropolitan Areas	Population				Growth					
					Number			%		
	1951	1956	1961	1966	1951-56	1956-61	1961-66	1951-56	1956-61	1961-66
Montreal	1,471,851	1,745,001	2,110,679	2,436,817	273,150	365,678	326,138	18.6	21.0	15.5
Toronto	1,210,353	1,504,277	1,824,589	2,158,496	293,924	320,312	333,907	24.3	21.3	18.3
Vancouver	561,960	665,017	790,165	892,286	103,057	125,148	102,121	18.3	18.8	12.9
Winnipeg	356,813	412,248	476,543	508,759	55,435	64,294	32,216	15.5	15.6	6.8
Ottawa—Hull	292,476	345,460	429,761	494,535	52,984	84,290	64,774	18.1	24.4	15.1
Hamilton	280,293	338,294	395,189	449,116	58,001	56,895	53,927	20.7	16.8	13.6
Quebec	276,242	311,604	357,568	413,397	35,362	45,964	55,829	12.8	14.8	15.6
Edmonton	176,782	254,800	337,568	401,299	78,018	82,768	63,731	44.1	32.5	18.9
Calgary	142,315	201,022	279,062	330,575	58,707	78,040	51,513	41.3	38.8	18.5
Windsor	163,618	185,865	193,365	211,697	22,067	7,500	18,332	13.6	4.0	9.5
London	128,977	154,453	181,283	207,396	25,476	26,830	26,113	19.8	17.4	14.4
Halifax	133,931	164,200	183,946	198,193	30,269	19,746	14,247	22.6	12.0	7.7
Kitchener	107,474	128,722	154,864	192,275	21,248	26,142	37,411	19.8	20.3	24.2
Victoria	113,207	133,829	154,152	173,455	20,622	20,323	19,303	18.2	15.2	12.5
Regina	71,319	89,755	112,176	131,127	18,436	22,421	18,951	25.9	25.0	16.9
Sudbury	73,826	97,945	110,799	117,075	24,119	12,854	6,276	32.7	13.1	5.7
Saskatoon	53,268	72,858	95,564	115,892	19,590	22,706	20,328	36.8	31.2	21.3
Saint John, N.B.	78,337	86,015	95,563	101,192	7,678	9,548	5,629	9.8	11.1	5.9
St. John's, Nfld.	68,620	79,153	91,654	101,161	10,533	12,501	9,507	15.3	15.8	10.4

Note: The Census Metropolitan Areas in this table are those as defined by the Dominion Bureau of Statistics.

The figures are for comparable areas for 1951-1956 and 1961-1966. Some boundary changes 1956-1961 added no more than 0.1% to the 1956 population except for St. John's where 1.0% of the 15.8% increase derived from an extension of the Census Metropolitan Area.

Sources:—Census of Canada, 1961, 1966
—Metropolitan Toronto Planning Board

4-43: POPULATION GROWTH AND SOURCE, CANADA, ONTARIO AND METROPOLITAN TORONTO PLANNING AREA 1951-1966

		Total Growth		Natural Increase		Net Migration	
		Population	%	Population	%	Population	%
Canada	1951-56	2,071,362	100	1,476,883	71	594,479	29
	1956-61	2,157,456	100	1,674,987	78	482,469	22
	1961-66	1,776,633	100	1,517,893	85	258,740	15
Ontario	1951-56	807,391	100	433,440	54	373,951	46
	1956-61	831,159	100	523,111	63	308,048	37
	1961-66	724,778	100	487,852	67	236,926	33
Metropolitan Toronto Planning Area	1951-56	280,343	100	103,786	37	176,557	63
	1956-61	302,047	100	143,986	48	158,061	52
	1961-66	322,512	100	147,906	46	174,606	54

Sources:—Census of Canada, Canadian Statistical Review, Immigration Statistics (Department of Manpower and Immigration—Ottawa)
—Metropolitan Toronto Planning Board
—For 1961-1966 Natural increase, M.T.P.B. estimates of births and deaths

4-44: POPULATION CHANGES BY CENSUS PERIODS, METROPOLITAN TORONTO PLANNING AREA AND SUB-GROUPS
1901-1966

Municipalities (1967 Boundaries)	BY TEN-YEAR PERIODS														BY FIVE-YEAR PERIODS					
	1901-11		1911-21		1921-31		1931-41		1941-51		1951-56		1956-61		1961-66	
	Change In No.	%	Change In No.	%	Change In No.	%	Change In No.	%	Change In No.	%	Change In No.	%	Change In No.	%	Change In No.	%
M.T.P.A.																
Periodic Change	+171,909	+65.3	+204,639	+47.0	+212,562	+33.2	+97,926	+11.5	+244,978	+25.8	+280,343	+23.5	+302,047	+17.0	+322,512	+18.1
Annual Change	+ 17,191	+ 5.2	+ 20,464	+ 3.9	+ 21,256	+ 2.9	+ 9,793	+ 1.1	+ 24,498	+ 2.3	+ 56,068	+ 4.3	+ 60,409	+ 3.8	+ 64,502	+ 3.4
MET. TOR.																
P.C.	+171,845	+72.2	+201,518	+49.2	+206,915	+33.8	+91,580	+11.2	+207,542	+22.8	+240,558	+21.5	+260,759	+19.2	+262,904	+16.2
A.C.	+ 17,185	+ 5.6	+ 20,152	+ 4.1	+ 20,692	+ 3.0	+ 9,158	+ 1.1	+ 20,754	+ 2.1	+ 48,111	+ 4.0	+ 52,152	+ 3.6	+ 52,581	+ 3.1
INNER 3																
P.C.	*	*	*	*	*	*	+68,219	+ 9.1	+ 70,241	+ 8.4	+ 18,818	+ 2.1	+ 23,815	+ 2.6	+ 5,731	+ 0.6
A.C.	*	*	*	*	*	*	+ 6,822	+0.87	+ 7,024	+0.81	+ 3,764	+0.42	+ 4,763	+0.52	+ 1,146	+0.12
MIDDLE 3																
P.C.	*	*	*	*	*	*	+23,361	+35.6	+138,301	+155.5	+221,742	+97.6	+236,944	+52.8	+257,183	+37.5
A.C.	*	*	*	*	*	*	+ 2,336	+ 3.1	+ 13,830	+9.84	+ 44,348	+14.59	+ 47,389	+8.85	+ 51,437	+6.58
FRINGE																
P.C.	+ 64	+0.03	+ 3,121	+12.3	+ 5,657	+19.8	+ 6,346	+18.6	+ 37,436	+92.3	+ 39,785	+51.0	+ 41,288	+35.1	+ 59,608	+37.5
A.C.	+ 6	+0.02	+ 312	+ 1.2	+ 566	+ 1.8	+ 635	+ 1.7	+ 3,744	+ 6.8	+ 7,957	+ 8.6	+ 8,258	+ 6.2	+ 11,921	+ 6.6
CITY OF TOR.																
P.C.	*	*	*	*	*	*	+44,757	+ 7.0	+ 12,929	+ 1.9	− 3,350	− 0.5	+ 6,743	+ 1.0	− 5,092	− 0.7

* Not available for 1967 Boundaries

Note: %'s for annual change are compound

Note: Inner 3 consists of the City of Toronto and the Boroughs of York and East York. Middle 3 consists of the Boroughs of Etobicoke, North York and Scarborough.
Fringe Area consists of all of the M.T.P.A. lying outside the Municipality of Metropolitan Toronto.

Sources: — Census of Canada
— Metropolitan Toronto Planning Board

4-45: POPULATION CHARACTERISTICS BY SELECTED CENSUS TRACTS*

Characteristics	From CBD** Westward Near & Along L. Ontario				From CBD Eastward Near and Along L. Ontario				From CBD Northward Along Yonge St. (W—West Side; E—East Side)			
	C.T. 60	C.T. 25	C.T. 147	C.T. 400	C.T. 99	C.T. 125	C.T. 171	C.T. 155	C.T. 91-E	C.T. 84-W	C.T. 199-E	C.T. 502 V. c Richmond H
Population, 1966	4,833	5,622	5,844	8,091	6,005	4,646	10,313	4,350	2,797	4,877	4,261	19,773
Age Group:												
Males	2,617	2,639	2,934	4,182	3,689	2,306	5,187	2,197	1,171	2,173	2,045	9,928
0— 4 years	259	223	282	541	223	239	466	322	60	155	241	1,205
5— 9 years	190	185	244	478	186	209	516	343	66	168	202	1,392
10—14 years	131	174	205	375	160	191	573	238	65	149	170	1,233
15—19 years	160	144	220	435	163	209	516	159	63	163	157	903
20—24 years	171	215	272	333	208	150	374	90	125	193	165	552
25—34 years	517	451	464	644	451	348	601	344	269	329	323	1,241
35—44 years	346	428	388	523	584	338	819	381	162	260	242	1,653
45—54 years	230	335	306	435	567	249	694	178	110	258	267	999
55—64 years	271	257	268	274	627	203	385	84	136	242	154	404
65—69 years	97	81	124	64	214	59	87	23	34	92	45	124
70 years and over	245	146	161	80	306	111	156	35	81	164	79	222
Females	2,216	2,983	2,910	3,909	2,316	2,340	5,126	2,153	1,626	2,704	2,216	9,845
0— 4 years	212	197	277	503	229	266	457	315	69	147	242	1,120
5— 9 years	213	183	230	428	192	226	511	334	55	145	191	1,357
10—14 years	141	167	201	373	151	207	499	230	51	117	155	1,137
15—19 years	126	222	223	348	129	184	473	125	77	177	175	806
20—24 years	226	403	274	341	175	175	352	90	194	209	186	563
25—34 years	397	419	386	568	333	282	623	404	224	348	317	1,381
35—44 years	262	432	340	520	308	305	857	334	184	354	283	1,694
45—54 years	211	291	340	415	296	255	651	154	199	366	296	895
55—64 years	211	287	301	239	223	215	363	93	212	349	178	391
65—69 years	90	118	137	77	117	62	134	31	111	179	61	179
70 years and over	127	264	201	97	163	163	206	43	250	313	132	322

*For Location of Census Tracts used in this table refer to map 4-18, page 48.   ** CBD — Central Business District

From CBD Northwestward				From CBD Northeastward				Additional Census Tracts (To Make A More Even Distribution of Samples)					Census Metropolitan Area
C.T. 37	C.T. 235	C.T.'s 139 + 305-T. Weston	C.T. 272	C.T. 106	C.T. 190	C.T. 281	C.T. 158	C.T. 1	C.T. 265	C.T. 219	C.T. 124	C.T. 191	
5,029	9,908	11,047	13,849	3,944	11,518	5,291	1,436	7,712	10,629	6,217	6,081	8,121	2,158,496
2,537	5,072	5,359	6,801	1,826	5,571	2,510	741	3,624	5,231	3,177	2,966	3,960	1,065,993
283	611	411	901	129	658	366	81	280	608	379	259	472	114,358
289	515	365	978	117	487	400	96	324	662	353	301	512	112,840
181	402	397	802	115	342	275	95	262	632	315	256	393	95,609
184	413	450	555	116	286	145	69	208	424	289	241	278	82,731
208	334	533	367	166	515	49	43	248	214	216	216	222	74,964
413	803	776	877	312	1,105	382	63	439	533	499	353	584	154,775
418	821	696	1,165	244	897	518	108	574	986	528	430	736	164,045
243	513	683	650	214	674	161	86	437	778	350	329	446	119,084
162	375	589	222	202	388	54	60	418	252	166	295	207	80,747
59	123	188	64	78	92	28	18	152	44	43	99	43	25,658
97	162	271	220	133	127	132	22	282	98	39	187	67	41,182
2,492	4,836	5,688	7,048	2,118	5,947	2,781	695	4,088	5,398	3,040	3,115	4,161	1,092,503
292	531	387	871	144	614	340	82	304	626	368	274	479	107,782
230	511	394	1,000	113	475	400	94	241	724	345	282	464	108,256
202	370	379	749	103	425	253	85	263	598	297	259	408	91,857
207	374	465	524	136	375	116	68	249	465	262	232	273	82,196
193	349	519	420	185	711	77	27	220	177	232	194	335	82,900
400	784	659	937	255	980	481	73	467	693	493	343	615	156,731
339	719	724	1,180	257	947	439	98	605	1,060	494	440	753	161,614
229	492	787	534	297	676	137	80	473	629	312	361	442	118,865
181	385	649	231	270	403	71	50	532	227	143	303	189	86,308
69	117	260	119	135	130	79	7	220	72	33	138	62	32,491
150	204	465	483	223	211	388	31	514	127	61	289	141	63,503

Source: Census of Canada, 1966

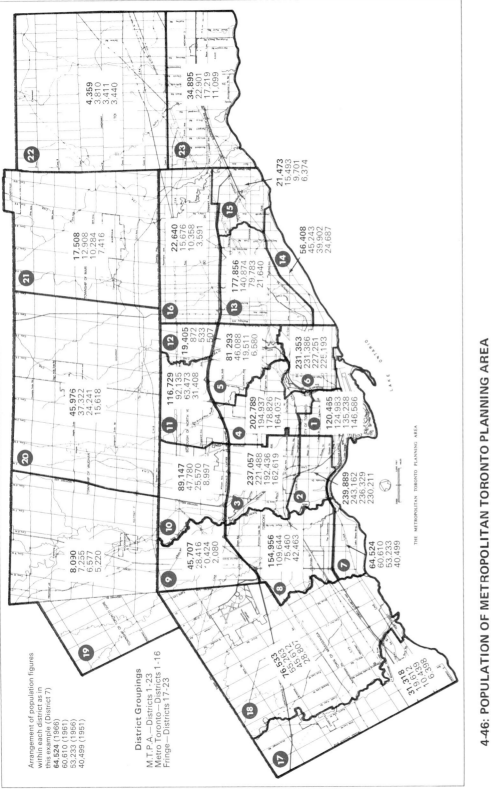

THE METROPOLITAN TORONTO PLANNING AREA

4-46: POPULATION OF METROPOLITAN TORONTO PLANNING AREA BY PLANNING DISTRICTS, 1966, 1961, 1956, 1951

Percentage of the total 1961 population
(of the particular area shown)
made up of immigrants who entered Canada
in the period 1946-1961

over 45%

30%-45%

0%-30%

Miles

4-47: IMMIGRANTS, 1946 TO 1961 (GREATLY GENERALIZED)

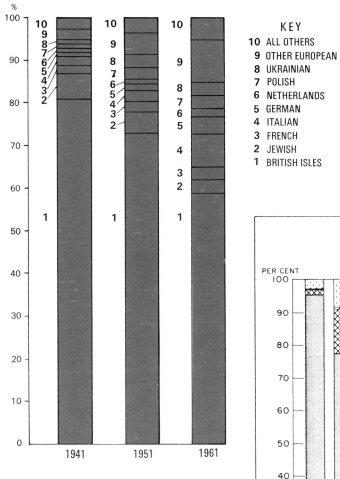

%

4-48: ETHNIC COMPOSITION,
METROPOLITAN TORONTO,
1941, 1951, 1961

KEY

10 ALL OTHERS
9   OTHER EUROPEAN
8   UKRAINIAN
7   POLISH
6   NETHERLANDS
5   GERMAN
4   ITALIAN
3   FRENCH
2   JEWISH
1   BRITISH ISLES

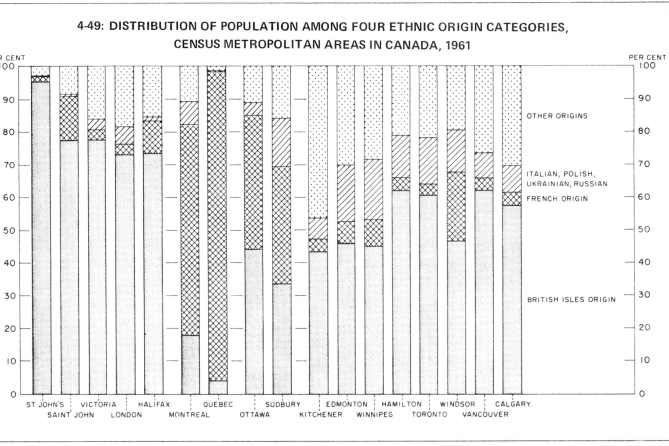

4-49: DISTRIBUTION OF POPULATION AMONG FOUR ETHNIC ORIGIN CATEGORIES,
CENSUS METROPOLITAN AREAS IN CANADA, 1961

OTHER ORIGINS

ITALIAN, POLISH,
UKRAINIAN, RUSSIAN

FRENCH ORIGIN

BRITISH ISLES ORIGIN

Source: Census of Canada, 1961

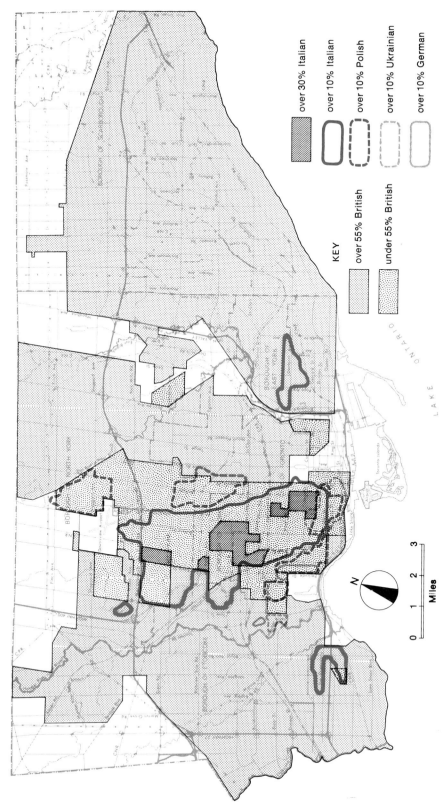

KEY

over 30% Italian
over 10% Italian
over 10% Polish
over 10% Ukrainian
over 10% German

KEY

over 55% British
under 55% British

N

Miles
0   1   2   3

4-50: ETHNIC GROUPS, METROPOLITAN TORONTO, 1961 (GREATLY GENERALIZED)

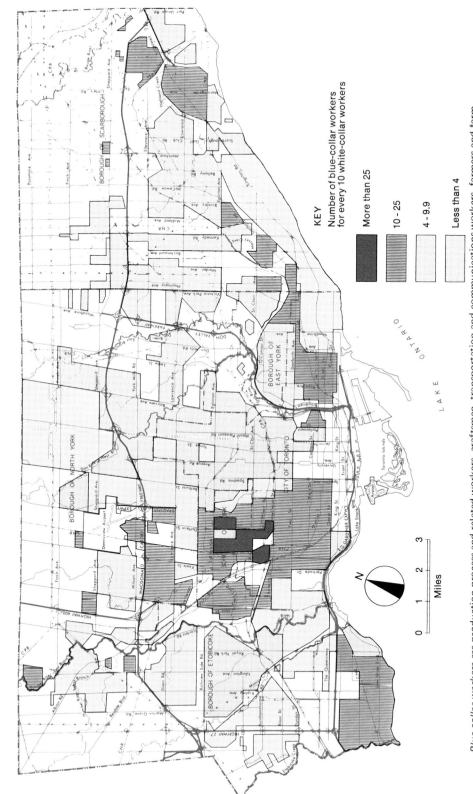

KEY

Number of blue-collar workers
for every 10 white-collar workers

More than 25
10 - 25
4 - 9.9
Less than 4

N

Miles
0   1   2   3

Blue-collar workers are production process and related workers, craftsmen, transportation and communications workers, farmers and farm workers, and labourers. *White-collar workers* are those in professional, managerial, technical, clerical, sales, services and recreation occupations. Map 4-51 indicates the number of blue-collar workers for every 10 white-collar workers by place of residence of the workers, not by place of employment.

4-52 LABOUR FORCE STATISTICS: Labour Force 14 years of age and over for 1951, 15 years of age and over for 1961

	TORONTO CENSUS METROPOLITAN AREA								ONTARIO							
	1951				1961				1951				1961			
	Male	Female	Total	%	Male	Female	Total	%	Male	Female	Total	%	Male	Female	Total	%
Agriculture, Forestry and Logging, Fishing and Trapping, Mining, Quarrying, Oil Wells	3,688	355	4,043	0.7	7,657	963	8,620	1.1	245,184	12,240	257,424	13.6	205,685	25,870	231,555	9.6
Manufacturing	138,812	50,459	189,271	35.9	170,615	63,896	234,511	29.7	489,448	125,910	615,358	32.6	504,624	138,660	643,284	26.8
Construction	35,701	968	36,669	7.0	49,174	1,881	51,055	6.5	124,884	2,610	127,494	6.7	149,293	4,573	153,866	6.4
Transport, Storage and Public Utilities	40,996	7,989	48,985	9.3	56,115	12,586	68,701	8.7	136,733	21,392	158,125	8.3	165,514	29,709	195,223	8.1
Trade	66,859	34,247	101,106	19.2	96,400	50,096	146,496	18.5	184,904	82,363	267,267	14.1	249,951	120,589	370,540	15.5
— Wholesale	24,437	7,611	32,048	6.1	37,667	11,927	49,594	6.3	52,308	12,521	64,829	3.4	82,536	20,197	102,733	4.3
— Retail	42,422	26,636	69,058	13.1	58,733	38,169	96,902	12.2	132,596	69,842	202,438	10.7	167,415	100,392	267,807	11.2
Finance, Insurance and Real Estate	16,823	14,902	31,725	6.1	27,000	25,338	52,338	6.6	32,992	28,736	61,728	3.2	51,303	47,151	98,454	4.1
Services	60,856	48,928	109,784	20.9	108,458	102,222	210,680	26.7	211,904	167,225	379,129	20.1	334,428	313,962	648,390	27.1
Not Stated	3,798	1,447	5,245	0.9	13,599	3,651	17,250	2.2	13,917	4,499	18,416	0.9	39,769	11,934	51,703	2.2
Total	367,533	159,295	526,828	100	529,018	260,633	789,651	100	1,439,966	444,975	1,884,941	100	1,700,567	692,448	2,393,015	100
	69.7%	30.3%	100%		67%	33%	100%		76.3%	23.7%	100%		71%	29%	100%	

Source: Census of Canada 1951, 1961

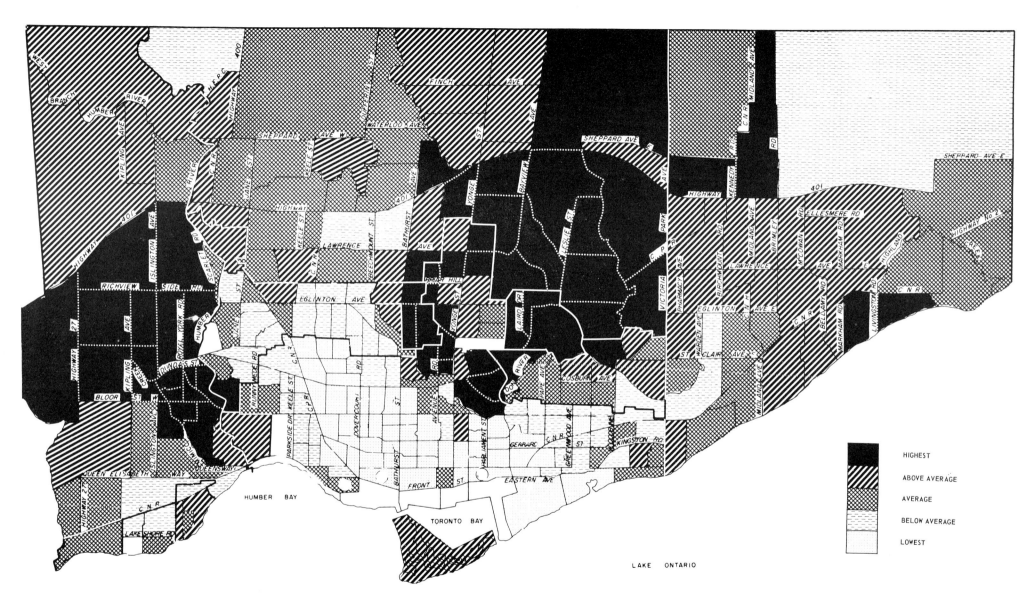

4-53: METROPOLITAN TORONTO AVERAGE FAMILY WAGE AND SALARY INCOMES, 1961

4. RESIDENTIAL LAND USE

In the preceding sections there are materials that reveal much about who the people of Toronto are, where they came from, how many there are and at what rate their number is increasing, what they do for a living, how they group themselves, and where they live. But these things do not tell anyone very much about the environment in which these people spend most of their non-working time and on which most of them spend a very high proportion of their income. We refer, of course, to the residential environment.

The purpose of this section is to provide some basic evidence of the degree of adequacy of housing in Toronto, how and why housing conditions differ from one part of the city to another and what can be done to improve these conditions.

Focal points
— The general pattern made by the distribution of residential land in the city
— The proportion of the city's total area taken up by residential land
— Relationships between
　　housing characteristics and income
　　housing characteristics and ethnic groups
　　housing characteristics and working class
　　housing characteristics and commercial-industrial patterns
　　housing characteristics and population density
　　housing characteristics and family characteristics
　　housing characteristics and features of the Toronto site
— Factors affecting the appearance and housing types of residential areas
— Trends in housing types in Toronto
— Housing problems

4-54: HOUSEHOLDS, FAMILIES AND HOUSING TYPES

	Census Metropolitan Area			City of Toronto		
	1951	1961	1966	1951	1961	1966
Households (Occupied Dwellings)	273,200	482,540	586,581	157,175	172,864	178,525
Families	302,381	466,495	534,734	177,984	162,916	153,206
Single Detached Dwellings	—	268,984	295,508	49,975	49,296	44,208
Single Attached Dwellings	—	84,385	95,428	—	60,450	55,763
Apartments and Flats	—	128,680	195,207	46,700	63,038	78,548

Source: Census of Canada, 1951, 1961, 1966

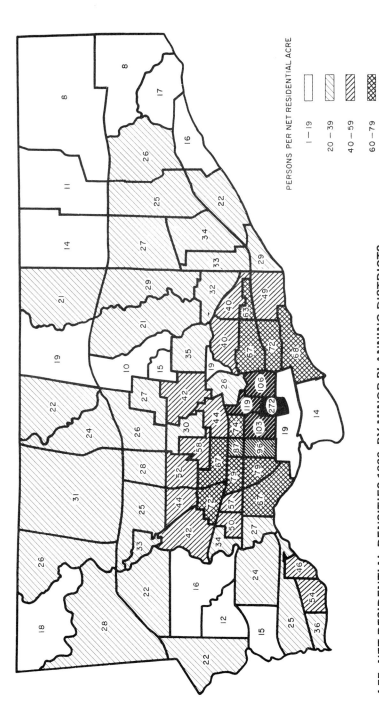

4-55: NET RESIDENTIAL DENSITIES 1966, BY MINOR PLANNING DISTRICTS

Note: Residential acreage in Map 4-55 includes the area covered by local roads.

PERSONS PER NET RESIDENTIAL ACRE

1 — 19　20 — 39　40 — 59　60 — 79　80 — 99　100 — 119　280

4-56: HOUSING CHARACTERISTICS BY SELECTED CENSUS TRACTS*, 1961

	CT 60	CT 25	CT 147	CT 400	CT 99	CT 125	CT 171	CT 155	CT 91	CT 84	CT 199	CT 502
Total Households (Occupied Dwellings)	1,398	1,168	1,713	1,732	1,676	1,140	2,150	777	942	1,705	1,253	4,045
Single Detached Dwellings	181	418	1,046	1,352	165	520	2,039	777	199	704	608	2,966
Apartments, Flats	463	438	560	152	904	142	—	—	568	593	615	288
Crowded Dwellings	251	125	156	252	339	137	215	—	—	—	—	428
Owner-occupied Dwellings	—	741	1,107	1,405	439	858	1,965	672	329	1,036	602	3,432
Median Value of Owner-occupied Dwellings	$ —	19,711	15,506	12,732	16,091	12,248	16,097	14,916	29,250	18,940	16,842	16,046
Tenant-occupied Dwellings	905	428	606	327	1,237	282	185	105	613	671	651	613
Average Rent of Tenant-occupied Dwellings	$ 71	106	93	82	74	97	96	78	116	109	110	105
Constructed Before 1920	1,260	884	202	127	1,525	451	—	—	469	250	—	301
Constructed Since 1945	—	—	513	1,005	—	219	1,850	673	145	233	1,189	3,542
In Need of Major Repair	200	—	—	111	108	—	—	—	—	—	—	—
Families	1,053	1,281	1,637	1,695	1,208	1,189	2,193	784	549	1,274	1,194	3,975
Persons per Family	3.2	3.0	3.1	3.8	3.1	3.4	3.7	3.8	3.0	3.0	3.3	3.9
Children per Family	1.2	1.0	1.1	1.8	1.1	1.4	1.7	1.8	1.0	1.0	1.3	1.9

Key
— Information not available

	CT 37	CT 235	CT 139	CT 272	CT 106	CT 190	CT 281	CT 158	CT 1	CT 265	CT 219	CT 124	CT 191	Census Metropolitan Area
Total Households (Occupied Dwellings)	1,021	2,563	2,851	3,083	1,207	2,388	1,131	359	2,287	2,032	1,346	1,662	2,296	482,540
Single Detached Dwellings	303	1,751	1,820	2,041	369	1,077	931	316	1,351	2,022	925	730	1,250	268,984
Apartments, Flats	202	579	831	892	450	1,216	200	—	639	—	378	261	964	128,680
Crowded Dwellings	195	461	143	326	—	109	—	—	142	—	185	190	104	47,311
Owner-occupied Dwellings	751	1,832	1,886	1,984	736	1,135	921	205	1,643	1,977	905	1,277	1,295	325,435
Median Value of Owner-occupied Dwellings	$14,921	13,504	16,657	17,419	20,483	21,863	16,348	19,230	19,381	21,240	15,766	14,716	19,850	17,301
Tenant-occupied Dwellings	270	731	965	1,099	471	1,253	210	154	644	—	441	385	1,001	157,055
Average Rent of Tenant-occupied Dwellings	$ 83	87	96	94	95	109	56	60	101	—	100	92	113	101
Constructed Before 1920	925	351	635	—	597	—	—	120	306	—	—	593	—	115,868
Constructed Since 1945	—	1,152	1,247	3,073	—	2,346	1,126	167	—	2,027	1,254	—	2,286	248,985
In Need of Major Repair	—	—	119	—	—	—	—	—	—	—	—	—	—	10,747
Families	1,194	2,671	2,578	2,976	1,042	2,278	1,034	339	2,225	2,059	1,464	1,684	2,210	466,495
Persons per Family	3.3	3.3	3.2	3.9	3.0	3.1	3.6	3.9	3.0	3.8	3.7	3.2	3.6	3.4
Children per Family	1.3	1.3	1.2	1.9	.9	1.1	1.6	1.9	.9	1.8	1.7	1.2	1.6	1.4

Source: Census of Canada, 1961 (Census Tracts in this table are the same as those in table 4-45, page 64 except for CT 139 which covers the area covered by CT 139 and CT 305 in 1966.)

*For location of Census Tracts used in this table refer to Map 4-18, page 48.

4-57: Part of the area covered by Census Tract 103, and adjacent areas

A Sub-Standard Area

4-58: Bright Street

4-59: HOUSING CHARACTERISTICS OF CENSUS TRACT 103, 1961

Total Households (Occupied Dwellings)	605
Single Detached Dwellings	104
Apartments, Flats	103
Crowded Dwellings	171
Owner-occupied Dwellings	—
Median Value of Owner-occupied Dwellings	—
Tenant-occupied Dwellings	352
Average Rent of Tenant-occupied Dwellings	$ 80
Constructed Before 1920	575
Constructed Since 1945	—
In Need of Major Repair	103
Families	603
Persons Per Family	4.1
Children Per Family	2.2

KEY

— Information
not
available

Source: Census of Canada, 1961

The Regent Park South Redevelopment Project

On January 31, 1947, the City of Toronto asked its electorate to vote on this question:

"Are you in favour of the City undertaking as a low cost or moderate cost rental housing project, with possible government assistance, the clearance, replanning, rehabilitation and modernization of the area bounded by Parliament, River, Gerrard and Dundas Streets, known as the Regent Park (North) Plan at an estimated cost of $5,900,000.00?"

In response to this question the "yes'es" outnumbered the "no's" 5 to 3 and the first redevelopment project of the National Housing Act was launched. That project was Regent Park North and it was a milestone in Canadian urban history.

In December 1953 the Council of the City of Toronto approved a resolution requesting the Federal and Provincial Governments' participation in the redevelopment of the area to the immediate south of Regent Park North. This area of approximately 26½ acres contained 458 houses (many housing more than one family) of which 219 were owner-occupied and 239 were tenant-occupied. The total population was 2,752. The area became known as Regent Park South.

Subsequently, a committee made up of representatives of the Provincial Government and the Central Mortgage and Housing Corporation made a careful preliminary survey of Regent Park South and presented to the Federal and Provincial Governments a set of recommendations, one of which read,

"That in view of the request of the City of Toronto the area known as Regent Park South, and defined earlier in this report, be considered sub-standard and, subject to certain listed exceptions, be cleared and redeveloped under the provisions of Sections 23 and 36 of the National Housing Act, and in accordance with the powers contained in the Ontario Housing Development Act."

In October 1954, a special task force known as the Joint Advisory Committee on Regent Park South was formed to study the area and prepare a detailed report and recommendations.

After interviewing 633 of the 638 families of the area, the committee found that,

57% wished to be relocated there
24% did not wish to be relocated
16% were undecided
3% did not answer

The report of the Joint Advisory Committee was submitted on January 31, 1955. It proposed that housing in the form of high-rise apartments and row houses totalling 721 units be constructed. The total estimated cost of acquiring and clearing the land was $4,679,874.00.

Source: Report of the Joint Advisory Committee on Regent Park South, January 31, 1955

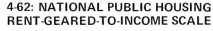

4-62: NATIONAL PUBLIC HOUSING RENT-GEARED-TO-INCOME SCALE

(Applies to Regent Park South)

Selected Monthly Family Income Categories	Old Scale Monthly Rent	New Scale* Monthly Rent
$	$	$
192	32	28
215	40	35
250	52	47
285	64	58
320	76	69
358	88	82
392	100	93
427	112	104
461	124	115
496	136	124
520	144	130
545	156	136
573	172	143

*Effective July 1, 1970

Source: Ontario Housing Corporation-Federal Rent-Income Scale

4-60: Regent Park in 1955

4-61: Regent Park in 1969

An Affluent Area

4-63: Residence, Census Tract 195

4-64: HOUSING CHARACTERISTICS OF CENSUS TRACT 195, 1961

Total Households (Occupied Dwellings)	146
Single Detached Dwellings	140
Apartments, Flats	—
Crowded Dwellings	—
Owner-occupied Dwellings	140
Median Value of Owner-occupied Dwellings	$37,500
Tenant-occupied Dwellings	—
Average Rent of Tenant-occupied Dwellings	—
Constructed Before 1920	—
Constructed Since 1945	—
In Need of Major Repair	—
Families	161
Persons Per Family	3.5
Children Per Family	1.5

Source: Census of Canada, 1961

KEY

— Information
not
available

4-65: Part of the area covered by Census Tract 195, and adjacent areas

4-66: Housing Types
A. Clarence Square: renovated row houses. These houses were erected in 1875 and formed part of a lower middle class area.
B. Single family dwellings in Leaside
C. Senior Citizens' apartments
D. Former workingmen's row houses, renovated into town houses
E. Condominium housing. In a condominium arrangement, a resident buys his dwelling unit and shares, with other residents in the building, the use of the surrounding property and other communal facilities.
F. Suburban single family dwelling
G. Older single family dwelling converted to university students' residence

a

b

c

d

e

f

g

4-67: HOUSING STARTS BY TYPE METROPOLITAN TORONTO

	Single Detached	Semi-detached & Duplex	Row	Apartment	Total	Apartment as % of Total
1958	9,934	1,558	N/A	12,809	24,301	53%
1960	4,145	1,400	79	8,556	14,180	60%
1962	5,827	1,852	843	8,024	16,546	48%
1964	8,014	2,392	1,704	16,700	28,810	58%
1966	7,246	1,732	1,646	11,531	22,155	52%
1968	5,555	1,745	2,280	28,195	37,775	75%

Source: Toronto Real Estate Board

4-68: METROPOLITAN TORONTO

AVERAGE PRICES OF NEW HOUSES

Survey Date	$16,000 and Under	Over $16,000 to $22,500	Over $22,500 to $30,000	Over $30,000	All Houses in Survey
July 15, 1963	9.0%	72.0%	15.0%	4.0%	$20,811
Jan. 15, 1965	12.0%	52.0%	18.0%	18.0%	$21,914
Jan. 31, 1968	.2%	13.8%	41.0%	45.0%	$32,361

Source: The Toronto Real Estate Board, Public Relations Department (D. B. Kirkup)
(Based on 500 units in each survey)

4-69: HOUSING STARTS PER 1,000 POPULATION IN SELECTED METROPOLITAN AREAS OF OVER 2,000,000

1967

	Housing Starts	Populations in thousands	Total Value Building Permits in millions	Starts per 1,000 population	Per Capita Construction Expenditure
Toronto, Ont.	32,038	2,117	$ 762.7	15.1	$360
Montreal, Que.	25,418	2,369	$ 475.1	10.7	$201
Washington, D.C.	24,113	2,408	$ 590.7	10.0	$245
Detroit, Mich.	27,497	3,987	$ 761.8	6.9	$191
Chicago, Ill.	41,080	6,689	$1,040.3	6.1	$156
Cleveland, Ohio	11,941	2,000	$ 365.6	5.9	$183
San-Francisco—Oakland, Cal.	15,567	2,918	$ 628.5	5.3	$215
Philadelphia, Pa.—N.J.	18,912	4,664	$ 459.9	4.1	$ 99
New York, N.Y.	42,624	11,366	$ 998.8	3.8	$ 88
Los Angeles—Long Beach, Cal.	22,154	6,765	$1,105.6	3.3	$163

Source: Toronto Real Estate Board

4-70: METROPOLITAN TORONTO
NUMBER AND AVERAGE PRICE OF MLS SALES BY DISTRICTS
TWELVE MONTHS—January to December
Houses only

DISTRICT	1966 (12 Months) No. of Sales	1966 (12 Months) Average Price	1968 (12 Months) No. of Sales	1968 (12 Months) Average Price
EAST				
E–1	765	$14,818	823	$18,732
E–2	512	$16,350	487	$21,141
E–3	640	$17,622	762	$22,589
E–4	414	$21,391	389	$27,103
E–5	180	$21,552	193	$29,658
E–6	362	$17,027	355	$22,495
E–7	339	$18,832	255	$25,238
E–8	626	$21,338	663	$26,791
E–9	485	$20,109	442	$26,690
E–10	151	$20,418	170	$26,700
E–11	6	$21,800	18	$30,786
WEST				
W–1	441	$20,260	352	$26,137
W–2	788	$19,932	625	$24,021
W–3	842	$18,494	644	$22,590
W–4	421	$22,737	364	$27,170
W–5	1127	$22,168	821	$27,671
W–6	327	$19,927	265	$23,235
W–7	182	$26,010	161	$31,117
W–8	625	$28,060	565	$35,124
W–9	279	$25,114	224	$32,644
W–10	423	$22,203	435	$27,974
CENTRAL				
C–1	576	$19,164	625	$24,167
C–2	683	$22,225	586	$27,283
C–3	500	$23,604	401	$29,239
C–4	208	$26,349	209	$32,186
C–5	242	$23,168	205	$29,108
C–6	137	$24,414	70	$33,753
C–7	201	$23,181	160	$28,560
C–8	92	$17,758	115	$20,633
C–9	49	$46,749	52	$54,748
C–10	131	$27,386	131	$33,160
C–11	36	$25,719	47	$32,984
C–12	147	$37,041	135	$44,288
C–13	124	$28,330	95	$39,418
C–14	148	$23,374	146	$29,979

Source: Toronto Real Estate Board

KEY

	Metro Area	Fringe Area
West	W 1-10	WF 1-4
Central	C 1-15	CF 1-2
East	E 1-11	EF 1-2

Source: Toronto Real Estate Board

Note: MLS stands for *Multiple Listing Service*. A person who wishes to sell his property can arrange through a member of the Toronto Real Estate Board to have a complete description and photograph of the property distributed to brokers and salesmen across the metropolitan area who are members of the Board.

4-71: MULTIPLE LISTING SERVICE SALES AREAS

4-72: METROPOLITAN TORONTO
MLS SALES AS % OF TOTAL MARKET

	TOTAL METRO MARKET Dollar Volume	Units	Average Price	MLS SALES Dollar Volume	Units	Average Price	MLS SALES as % of Total Metro Market
1966	$1,096,306,168	41,907	$26,160	$326,687,333	14,883	$21,950	29.8%
1968	$1,045,017,320	34,600	$30,203	$430,301,604	15,570	$27,637	41.2%

Source: Toronto Real Estate Board

Housing Needs

For people to live satisfactorily they must be adequately housed. Moreover, the cost of their housing should be low enough that they are not paying an unreasonable proportion of their income for their shelter. But what is "adequate" housing? And what is a "reasonable" proportion of one's income? Certainly, not everyone would have the same views on these matters. Nevertheless, planners and others engaged in urban research have developed some general guidelines that are valuable in helping us gain some idea of what adequate housing and reasonable housing costs might be.

In a report commissioned by the Metropolitan Toronto Planning Board in 1969, a housing unit was considered inadequate if it could be classified in any of the following four categories:

1. In poor structural condition either alone or in combination with overcrowding (occupancy of a dwelling unit by more than one person per room)
2. In poor condition and occupied by two or more families, either with or without overcrowding
3. Occupied by two or more families either with or without overcrowding
4. Overcrowded

Housing units not classified in any of these four categories were considered adequate.

In the same report, a housing cost table or scale, developed by the Central Mortgage and Housing Corporation (CMHC) and adopted by the Ontario Housing Corporation (OHC) was used to determine whether or not housing costs were within or beyond a reasonable proportion of a person's or a family's income. This scale was based on what CMHC and OHC felt was a reasonable amount of rent for fully serviced (heat, water, stove, and refrigerator) public housing units—units, that is, provided by governmental agencies. Many people, of course, do not pay rent, in the strictest sense, because they buy their houses, but the amount of money it costs them to pay for their houses and keep them in good condition could, in a sense, be considered as "rent." Therefore, the same scale can be used fairly reliably for them as for the true renters. The following two cases taken from the scale give an idea of the way the scale relates rent to income. A family with a total income of $200.00 per month, for example, would be expected to pay $35.00 rent per month, or 17.5% of its total income.

On the other hand, a family with a total income of $500.00 per month would be expected to pay $137.00 rent per month or 27.4% of its total income. As you can see, the more money a family makes, the greater is the proportion of its income that should go into rent or housing costs. (In 1970 OHC adopted a new scale. The basic features of this scale are indicated in Table 4-62, page 74.)

These guidelines for adequate housing and housing costs were used in calculating the figures presented in Table 4-73. This table gives some idea of what the needs for housing in the Metropolitan Toronto Planning Area were in the recent past and what they were forecasted to be by 1981. The figures used are figures of shelter units. A *shelter unit* is the accommodation occupied by a family or a non-family individual.

4-73: HOUSING NEEDS IN THE METROPOLITAN TORONTO PLANNING AREA*, 1961-1981

	1961		1966		Shelter Units Needed to Eliminate 1966 Inadequacies		Shelter Units Needed To Accommodate Population Growth, and Losses in Stock From 1966 to 1981		Total No. of New Shelter Units Needed To Overcome the 1966 Backlog and Provide for Growth and Losses in Stock By 1981	
	Number	%	Number	%	Number	%	Number	%	Number	%
All Families and Non-Family Individuals (= Shelter Units)	670,367	100	771,913	100	59,429	100	361,999	100	421,428	100
Able to Find Adequate Shelter Within their Incomes	297,184	44	411,160	53			163,435	45	163,435	39
Unable to Find Adequate Shelter Within their Incomes—Total	373,183	56	360,753	47	59,429	100	198,564	55	257,993	61
1. Eligible for Public Housing	53,759	8	46,289	6	24,184	41	99,309	28	123,493	29
a) Family Type Units	40,333	6	34,889	5	17,878	30	77,608	22	95,486	23
b) Elderly Persons' Units	13,426	2	11,400	1	6,306	11	21,701	6	28,007	6
2. Not Eligible for Public Housing	319,424	48	314,464	41	35,245	59	99,255	27	134,500	32
a) Shelter Adequate but Beyond Income	229,842	34	237,116	31						
b) Shelter Inadequate	89,582	14	77,348	10	35,245	59				

Note: The "FORECAST" heading spans the last three header groups (Shelter Units Needed to Eliminate 1966 Inadequacies, Shelter Units Needed To Accommodate Population Growth..., Total No. of New Shelter Units Needed...).

Source: *Housing Needs in The Metropolitan Toronto Planning Area* — A Report by Paterson Planning and Research Ltd. for The Metropolitan Toronto Planning Board, 1969.
*For the Extent of The Metropolitan Toronto Planning Area Refer to Map 4-46, Page 66.

5. TRANSPORTATION

The modern city could not exist, indeed, never would have developed, without transportation. A transportation network is the circulation system that connects a city with other places (thus defining, to a considerable degree, the city's situation) and moves people and goods in the interior of the city to and from the thousands of points where the activities that characterize urban life are carried on. In other words, specialized areas of land use in the city are formed in large measure by transportation developments. These areas, then, are the products of transportation and, at the same time, basic generators of movement within the city.

We must recognize, also, that transportation facilities take up large amounts of land, and form, themselves, a major element in the general land use picture.

Focal points

- The general characteristics of Toronto's transportation network
- The effects of the Toronto site on transportation patterns
- The effects of decisions made early in Toronto's history on the present-day transportation network
- The accessibility of the city core and the capacity of the core to meet parking demands
- Principal periods and areas of traffic congestion
- Developments and trends in methods of transportation, volume of traffic, and the basic transportation network of Toronto
- The location of airports and their effects on land use patterns around them; the effects of surrounding land use patterns on airports
- Relationships between the various forms and routes of transportation
- The effects of transportation routes on the growth of Toronto
- Ways in which the various land uses generate traffic patterns
- The advantages, disadvantages, and relative importance of the various forms of transportation
- The expressway controversy
- The capability of Toronto's transportation network to meet traffic conditions
- Solutions to traffic problems

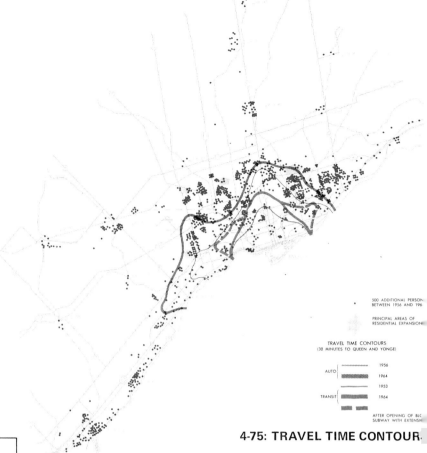

4-75: TRAVEL TIME CONTOUR

500 ADDITIONAL PERSON BETWEEN 1956 AND 196

PRINCIPAL AREAS OF RESIDENTIAL EXPANSION

TRAVEL TIME CONTOURS
(30 MINUTES TO QUEEN AND YONGE)

AUTO
1956
1964

TRANSIT
1953
1964
AFTER OPENING OF BLC SUBWAY WITH EXTENSION

4-76: LOCATION OF DOWNTOWN AND INTERMEDIATE CORDON

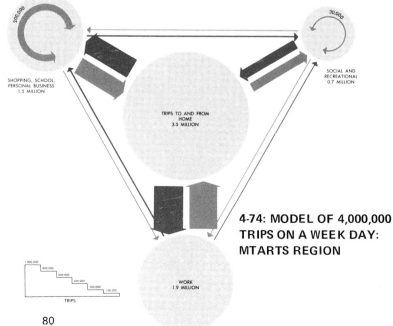

4-74: MODEL OF 4,000,000 TRIPS ON A WEEK DAY: MTARTS REGION

In the area established for analysis by the Metropolitan Toronto and Region Transportation Study—the MTARTS Region (see map accompanying Diagram 7-2, page 112)—approximately 4,000,000 trips were undertaken on a typical weekday in 1964. Diagram 4-74 is a model that illustrates the basic patterns made by those trips. Four groups of activities are represented by the circles shown. (The only school trips represented are those that were made in a vehicle.) Each circle is proportional in area to the number of arrivals at, plus departures from, that activity. The arrows linking the circles are proportional in width to the number of trips between given pairs of activity groups. The arrows within the top two circles represent the number of trips whose origins and destinations are both in the same activity group. A small scale is provided for estimating the number of trips that each arrow represents.

80

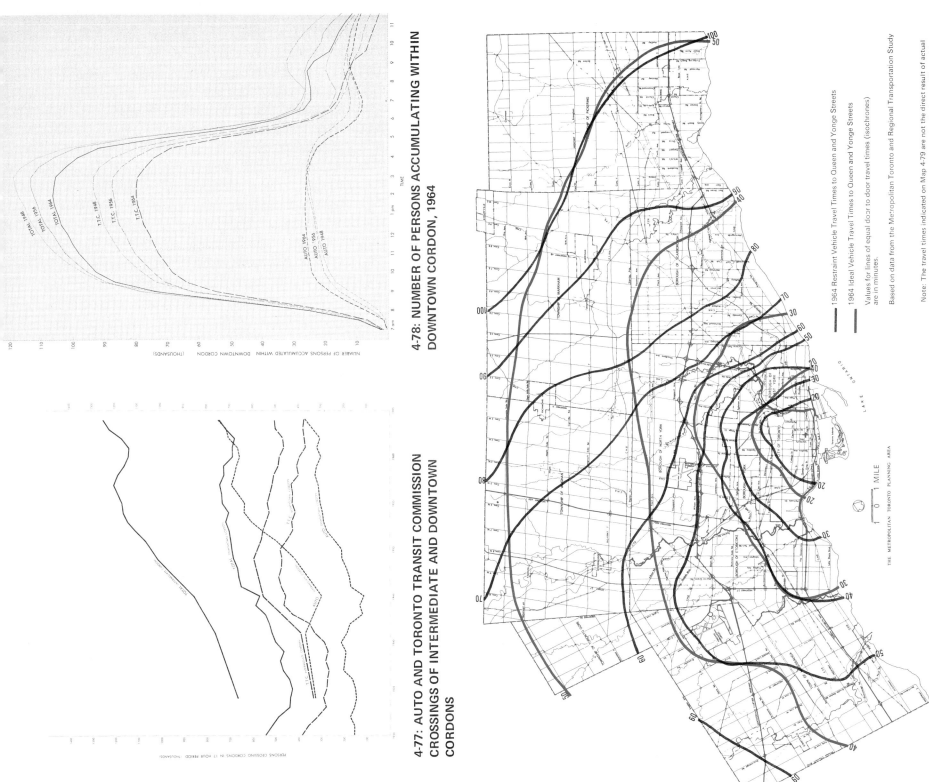

4-77: AUTO AND TORONTO TRANSIT COMMISSION CROSSINGS OF INTERMEDIATE AND DOWNTOWN CORDONS

4-78: NUMBER OF PERSONS ACCUMULATING WITHIN DOWNTOWN CORDON, 1964

4-79: VEHICLE TRAVEL TIMES TO QUEEN AND YONGE STREETS, 1964

1964 Restraint Vehicle Travel Times to Queen and Yonge Streets

1964 Ideal Vehicle Travel Times to Queen and Yonge Streets

Values for lines of equal door to door travel times (isochrones) are in minutes.

Based on data from the Metropolitan Toronto and Regional Transportation Study

Note: The travel times indicated on Map 4-79 are not the direct result of actual measurements of traffic flow. The times were calculated using a traffic model and a computer. **Restraint Vehicle Travel Times** were the result of calculations based on expected travel conditions along the various routes; **Ideal Vehicle Travel Times** were based on hypothetical conditions under which traffic could flow freely along the various routes.

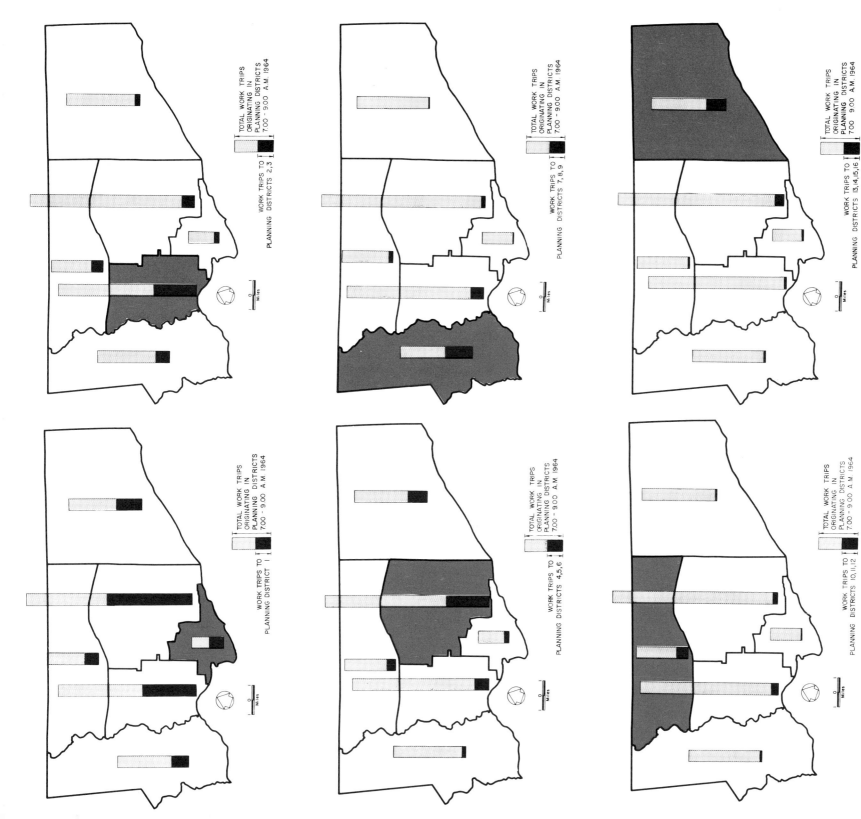

TOTAL WORK TRIPS
ORIGINATING IN
PLANNING DISTRICTS
7:00 - 9:00 A.M. 1964

WORK TRIPS TO
PLANNING DISTRICT 1

TOTAL WORK TRIPS
ORIGINATING IN
PLANNING DISTRICTS
7:00 - 9:00 A.M. 1964

WORK TRIPS TO
PLANNING DISTRICTS 4,5,6

TOTAL WORK TRIPS
ORIGINATING IN
PLANNING DISTRICTS
7:00 - 9:00 A.M. 1964

WORK TRIPS TO
PLANNING DISTRICTS 10,11,12

Scale for total
number of work trips

30,000 total
work trips

TOTAL WORK TRIPS
ORIGINATING IN
PLANNING DISTRICTS
7:00 - 9:00 A.M. 1964

WORK TRIPS TO
PLANNING DISTRICTS 2,3

TOTAL WORK TRIPS
ORIGINATING IN
PLANNING DISTRICTS
7:00 - 9:00 A.M. 1964

WORK TRIPS TO
PLANNING DISTRICTS 7,8,9

TOTAL WORK TRIPS
ORIGINATING IN
PLANNING DISTRICTS
7:00 - 9:00 A.M. 1964

WORK TRIPS TO
PLANNING DISTRICTS 13,14,15,16

4-80: WORK TRIP DISTRIBUTIONS

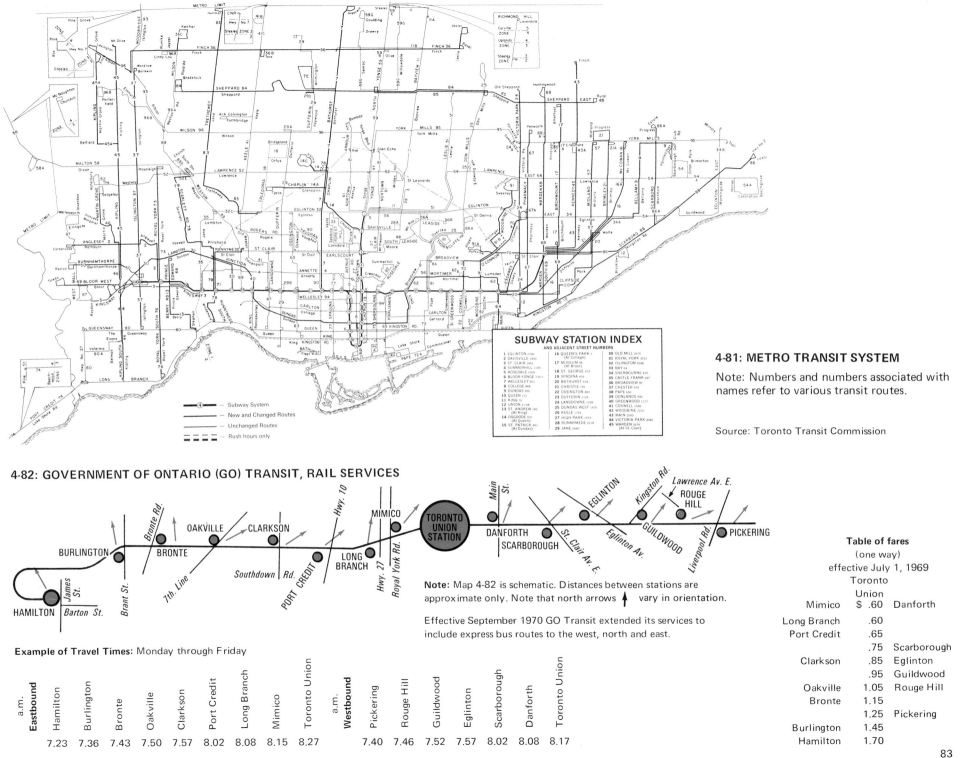

SUBWAY STATION INDEX
AND ADJACENT STREET NUMBERS

1 EGLINTON 2200	16 QUEEN'S PARK 1 (At College)	30 OLD MILL 2676
2 DAVISVILLE 1900	17 MUSEUM 95 (At Bloor)	31 ROYAL YORK 3012
3 ST. CLAIR 1441	18 ST. GEORGE 323	32 ISLINGTON 3266
4 SUMMERHILL 1189	19 SPADINA 403	33 BAY 64
5 ROSEDALE 1009	20 BATHURST 558	34 SHERBOURNE 420
6 BLOOR-YONGE 733-1	21 CHRISTIE 735	35 CASTLE FRANK 687
7 WELLESLEY 551	22 OSSINGTON 883	36 BROADVIEW 90
8 COLLEGE 448	23 DUFFERIN 1126	37 CHESTER 370
9 DUNDAS 300	24 LANSDOWNE 1299	38 PAPE 650
10 QUEEN 171	25 DUNDAS WEST 1525	39 DONLANDS 990
11 KING 76	26 KEELE 1733	40 GREENWOOD 1177
12 UNION 21-48	27 HIGH PARK 1874	41 COXWELL 1568
13 ST. ANDREW 140 (At King)	28 RUNNYMEDE 2218	42 WOODBINE 2076
14 OSGOODE 320 (At Queen)	29 JANE 2440	43 MAIN 2550
15 ST. PATRICK 481 (At Dundas)		44 VICTORIA PARK 3060
		45 WARDEN 3276 (At St. Clair)

Legend:
- Subway System
- New and Changed Routes
- Unchanged Routes
- Rush hours only

4-81: METRO TRANSIT SYSTEM

Note: Numbers and numbers associated with names refer to various transit routes.

Source: Toronto Transit Commission

4-82: GOVERNMENT OF ONTARIO (GO) TRANSIT, RAIL SERVICES

Note: Map 4-82 is schematic. Distances between stations are approximate only. Note that north arrows ↑ vary in orientation.

Effective September 1970 GO Transit extended its services to include express bus routes to the west, north and east.

Example of Travel Times: Monday through Friday

a.m. Eastbound	Hamilton	Burlington	Bronte	Oakville	Clarkson	Port Credit	Long Branch	Mimico	Toronto Union
	7.23	7.36	7.43	7.50	7.57	8.02	8.08	8.15	8.27

a.m. Westbound	Pickering	Rouge Hill	Guildwood	Eglinton	Scarborough	Danforth	Toronto Union
	7.40	7.46	7.52	7.57	8.02	8.08	8.17

Table of fares
(one way)
effective July 1, 1969

Toronto Union		
Mimico	$ .60	Danforth
Long Branch	.60	
Port Credit	.65	
	.75	Scarborough
Clarkson	.85	Eglinton
	.95	Guildwood
Oakville	1.05	Rouge Hill
Bronte	1.15	
	1.25	Pickering
Burlington	1.45	
Hamilton	1.70	

4-83: PEAK TRAVEL DEMAND, MTARTS REGION, 1964 (DESIRE LINES)

40 20

PERSON TRIPS
(BOTH WAYS, IN THOUSANDS)
ALL MODES COMBINED
MORNING PEAK

Maps 4-83 and 4-84 show the general patterns of morning peak period (7 a.m. to 9 a.m.) travel demand in the MTARTS Region and in Metropolitan Toronto. The solid lines on the maps are called desire lines. A *desire line* is a straight line connecting two points on a map and represents a demand (or desire) for travel between those two points. Desire lines do not represent existing transportation routes, but indicate the general direction in which people would move if they were free to do so. The width of a desire line is proportional to the volume of travel demand that exists between the two points concerned: the greater the demand, the wider the line. Both the MTARTS Region and Metropolitan Toronto were subdivided into small areas for purposes of analysis. These small areas are shown by broken lines on the maps. In each area a traffic node or central point is indicated. The network of desire lines connecting the nodes indicates the pattern of medium- and long-distance trips in the morning peak and allows one to visualize to what extent ideal traffic routing would differ from the actual routes imposed by the existing road and transit systems.

40 20

PERSON TRIPS
(BOTH WAYS, IN THOUSANDS)
ALL MODES COMBINED
MORNING PEAK

4-84: PEAK TRAVEL DEMAND, METRO, 1964 (DESIRE LINES)

4-85: TRAFFIC FLOW, MTARTS REGION, 1964

VEHICLE FLOWS
(BOTH WAYS - IN THOUSANDS)
24 HOURS

VEHICLE FLOWS
(BOTH WAYS - IN THOUSANDS)
24 HOURS

4-86: TRAFFIC FLOW, METRO, 1964

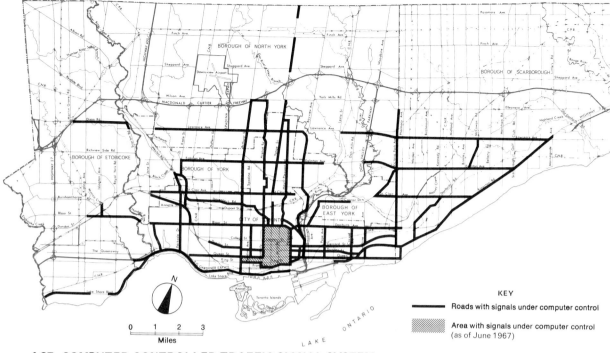

4-87: COMPUTER-CONTROLLED TRAFFIC SIGNAL SYSTEM

KEY

— Roads with signals under computer control

▨ Area with signals under computer control (as of June 1967)

4-88: PARKING SPACES IN THE DOWNTOWN CORE*

Year	Public Parking		Private Parking		Total	Motor Vehicle Registration In Metropolitan Toronto
	Garage	Lot	Garage	Lot		
1938	4,895	7,826	—	1,696	14,417	
1959	5,737	7,178	832	3,042	16,789	498,273
1961	6,159	7,008	979	3,103	17,249	558,618

Don Valley Parkway opened—Bloor Street to Eglinton Avenue

1962	5,850	6,652	1,083	3,139	16,724	574,102

Gardiner Expressway opened—York Street to Humber River

1963	6,910	7,552	1,003	2,999	18,464	594,343
1965	7,562	7,009	1,372	2,025	17,968	632,910

Gardiner Expressway opened—York Street to Leslie Street

1967	7,695	7,588	1,384	2,116	18,783	691,949
1968	7,031	7,554	1,017	3,058	18,660	784,940
1969	7,384	7,909	1,324	2,032	18,649	

*Defined for these purposes as the area bounded by Simcoe St., Dundas St., Front St., and Jarvis St.

Sources: Metropolitan Toronto Roads and Traffic Department and Department of Transport, Ontario

4-89: Toronto International Airport

4-90: The Bloor Street viaduct over the Don valley

LAWRENCE AVENUE

EGLINTON AVENUE

(Toronto is on the brink of repeating the mistakes of Los Angeles), "where at rush hour the cars on the great freeways crawl at 10 m.p.h., where the poor have no practical way to reach jobs, where the exhausts have turned the air into a crisis, where expressways, interchanges, and parking lots occupy some two-thirds of the drained and vacuous downtown."

From *The Death and Life of Great American Cities,* Jane Jacobs, Random House, Inc., 1961

"When reports went to the Council extolling the virtues of our expressway system, why did these reports not also include information on the number of houses that would have to be torn down? The acres of public parkland that would be used up? The number of people who would have to live next door to the expressway? And the number of additional cars (as many as 4,000 an hour at the peak periods) that would be expected on the old-fashioned downtown street system?"

From *The Bad Trip, The Untold Story of the Spadina Expressway,* David and Nadine Nowlan, House of Anansi and New Press, 1970

". . . the world's most supercolossal carsophagus."

Marshall McLuhan

4-91, 4-92: The Spadina (William R. Allen) Expressway under construction

The *Globe and Mail,* Toronto

Source: Metropolitan Toronto Planning Board

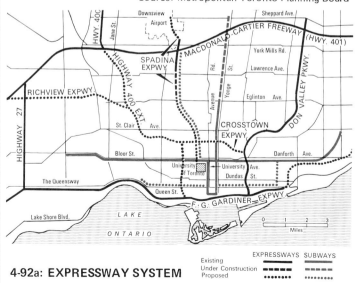

4-92a: EXPRESSWAY SYSTEM

	EXPRESSWAYS	SUBWAYS
Existing		
Under Construction		
Proposed		

"You could build subway stations right in the backyards of some people, and they'd still drive their cars. It may be the ease, the convenience, the privacy. But no matter, that's their choice . . .

"Look at the spectacular skyscraper development in downtown Toronto; look at the apartment towers rising against the sky out to the very limits of Metro; look at the dispersal of office buildings to suburban areas like Flemingdon Park; look at the distribution of industries all over Metro. How, I ask the protesters, is the movement of people, and goods, going to take place among these components except by a well-balanced transportation system, including a rapid transit and expressways?"

Frederick G. Gardiner in the *Toronto Daily Star,* Saturday, March 7, 1970

"Good morning. Henry Shannon in the CFRB jet traffic helicopter over the Highway 27-401-Airport Expressway area and the traffic below is normal. At the Richview Side Road, though, we have that construction situation there again, as we have had for a few days. South on Highway 27, then, is noticeably slow from south of the Richview Side Road and until you get around Rathburn Road where it starts to get a little better. For the rest of the city we have the normal buildup so far. And now back to the Studio."

"Good evening. This is Henry Shannon in the CFRB jet traffic helicopter and we're looking over the Don Valley Parkway. Where I am at Pottery Road it looks fine, but, hold on, we've discovered something. Yes, just below the Bloor Viaduct in the northbound lanes it is very slow indeed. It looks like, yes, we have a truck to the right of the road and also two other cars blocking the righthand lane. This is immediately below the Bloor Viaduct. Now that traffic is really starting to back up and, of course, people are slowing down to take a look. It's the old rubberneck situation—something that we can't seem to stop because it's a human frailty and because of this that traffic is backed up now to well south of the Gerrard Overpass. It's backing up a bit more as each minute goes by. My suggestion is avoid the bottom end of the Don Valley Parkway; take the Bayview Extension and also O'Connor Drive and Broadview. They look okay. And now back to the Studio."

Courtesy Henry Shannon and CFRB Radio

4-93: Transportation routes and other land use patterns in and around the Leaside manufacturing area

6. OTHER LAND USE PATTERNS

The materials on the next few pages present information about several important facilities. These facilities can be considered as major land uses, but they do not form patterns that can be analyzed as intensively as the patterns on the previous pages. For this reason they have been grouped into one section. This does not mean they should be treated lightly: there are many aspects of their functions and distribution that deserve close attention.

Focal points
- The situation of Toronto with respect to hydro-electric power sources; advantages of the Toronto site for thermal and nuclear power developments
- The proportion of land in Toronto that parks and conservation areas account for
- Relationships between parks and conservation areas and features of the site of the Toronto area; relationships between parks and conservation areas and other land use patterns
- The accessibility of the parks and recreation facilities to the residents of Toronto
- Relationships between water supply systems and sewerage systems and site
- Relationships between water supply systems and the transportation network
- Water supply system and sewerage systems as indicators of growth in Toronto
- The number and variety of educational facilities that a large city provides
- Distribution patterns of the various educational facilities
- Relationships between the distribution of educational facilities and population distribution and other land uses
- The advantages, disadvantages and problems of a downtown university campus
- The characteristics of the landscape within and adjacent to the University of Toronto-Government buildings complex

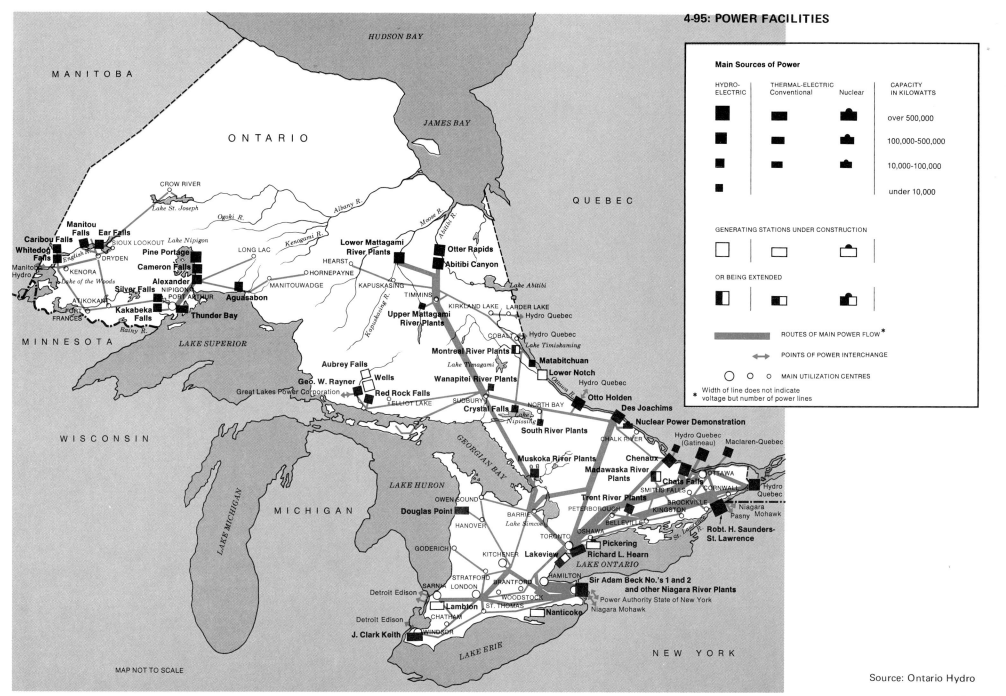

4-95: POWER FACILITIES

HUDSON BAY

MANITOBA

ONTARIO

JAMES BAY

QUEBEC

Main Sources of Power

HYDRO-ELECTRIC	THERMAL-ELECTRIC Conventional	Nuclear	CAPACITY IN KILOWATTS
■	■	♠	over 500,000
■	■	♠	100,000-500,000
■	■	♠	10,000-100,000
■			under 10,000

GENERATING STATIONS UNDER CONSTRUCTION

□   □   ◐

OR BEING EXTENDED

◧   ◧   ◧

ROUTES OF MAIN POWER FLOW *

POINTS OF POWER INTERCHANGE

◯ ◦ ∘ MAIN UTILIZATION CENTRES

* Width of line does not indicate voltage but number of power lines

CROW RIVER

Lake St. Joseph

Ogoki R.   Albany R.   Moose R.   Abitibi R.

Lake Nipigon

LONG LAC

Kenogami R.

Manitou Falls   **Ear Falls**   SIOUX LOOKOUT

Caribou Falls

Whitedog Falls   English R.   DRYDEN   **Pine Portage**   HEARST   **Lower Mattagami River Plants**   **Otter Rapids**

Manitoba Hydro   KENORA   **Cameron Falls**   ○HORNEPAYNE   **Abitibi Canyon**

Lake of the Woods   **Alexander**   MANITOUWADGE   KAPUSKASING   Lake Abitibi

ATIKOKAN   **Silver Falls**   NIPIGON   PORT ARTHUR   TIMMINS   Hydro Quebec

FORT FRANCES   **Kakabeka Falls**   **Aguasabon**   KIRKLAND LAKE   LARDER LAKE   Hydro Quebec

Thunder Bay   **Upper Mattagami River Plants**   Hydro Quebec

MINNESOTA   Rainy R.   LAKE SUPERIOR   COBALT   Hydro Quebec

Lake Timiskaming

Montreal River Plants

Aubrey Falls   Lake Timagami   **Matabitchuan**

WISCONSIN   **Geo. W. Rayner**   **Wells**   **Wanapitei River Plants**   **Lower Notch**   Ottawa R.   Hydro Quebec

Great Lakes Power Corporation   **Red Rock Falls**   **Otto Holden**

ELLIOT LAKE   SUDBURY   NORTH BAY   **Des Joachims**

Crystal Falls   Lake Nipissing   **Nuclear Power Demonstration**

South River Plants   CHALK RIVER

Hydro Quebec (Gatineau)   Maclaren-Quebec

GEORGIAN BAY   **Muskoka River Plants**   **Chenaux**

Madawaska River Plants   **Chats Falls**   OTTAWA   Hydro Quebec

LAKE HURON   OWEN SOUND   **Trent River Plants**   SMITHS FALLS   CORNWALL

LAKE MICHIGAN   **Douglas Point**   HANOVER   PETERBOROUGH   BROCKVILLE   Niagara Pasny   Mohawk

MICHIGAN   BARRIE   Lake Simcoe   BELLEVILLE   KINGSTON   **Robt. H. Saunders-St. Lawrence**

GODERICH   TORONTO   OSHAWA   St. Lawrence R.

KITCHENER   **Lakeview**   **Pickering**

STRATFORD   **Richard L. Hearn**   LAKE ONTARIO

SARNIA   LONDON   BRANTFORD   HAMILTON   **Sir Adam Beck No.'s 1 and 2 and other Niagara River Plants**

Detroit Edison   WOODSTOCK   ST. THOMAS   Power Authority State of New York   Niagara Mohawk

Lambton   CHATHAM

Detroit Edison   **Nanticoke**

J. Clark Keith   WINDSOR

LAKE ERIE   NEW YORK

MAP NOT TO SCALE

Source: Ontario Hydro

89

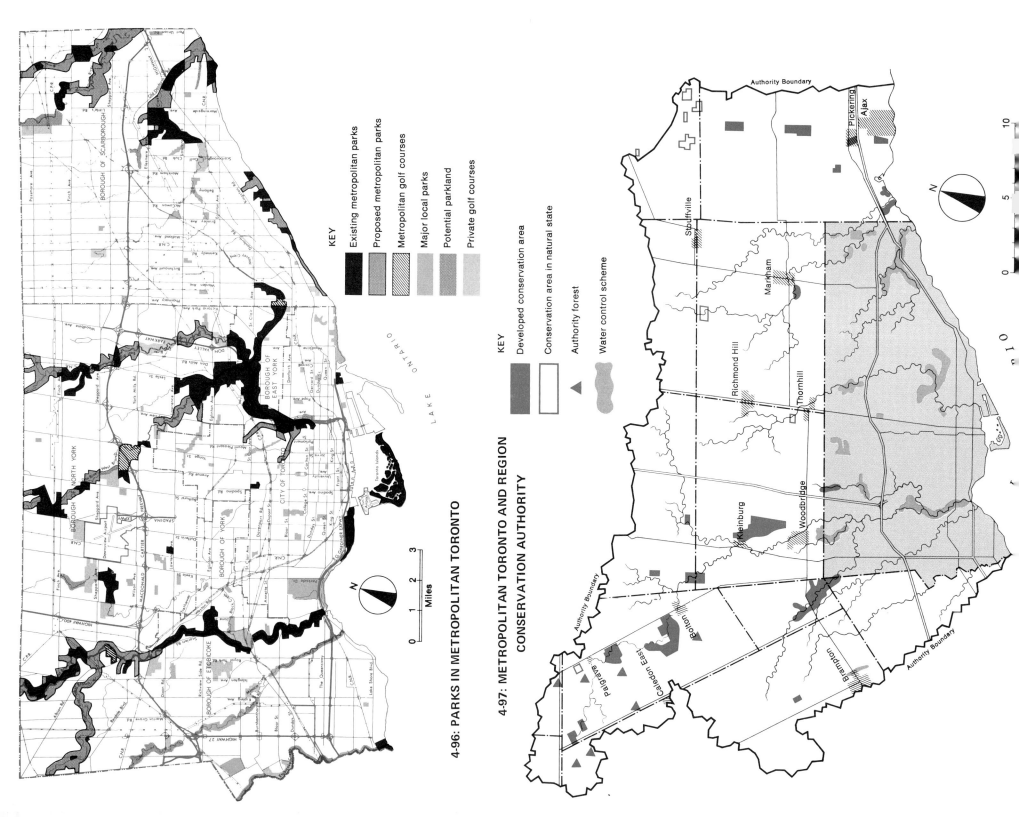

KEY

Existing metropolitan parks
Proposed metropolitan parks
Metropolitan golf courses
Major local parks
Potential parkland
Private golf courses

4-96: PARKS IN METROPOLITAN TORONTO

KEY

Developed conservation area
Conservation area in natural state
Authority forest
Water control scheme

4-97: METROPOLITAN TORONTO AND REGION
CONSERVATION AUTHORITY

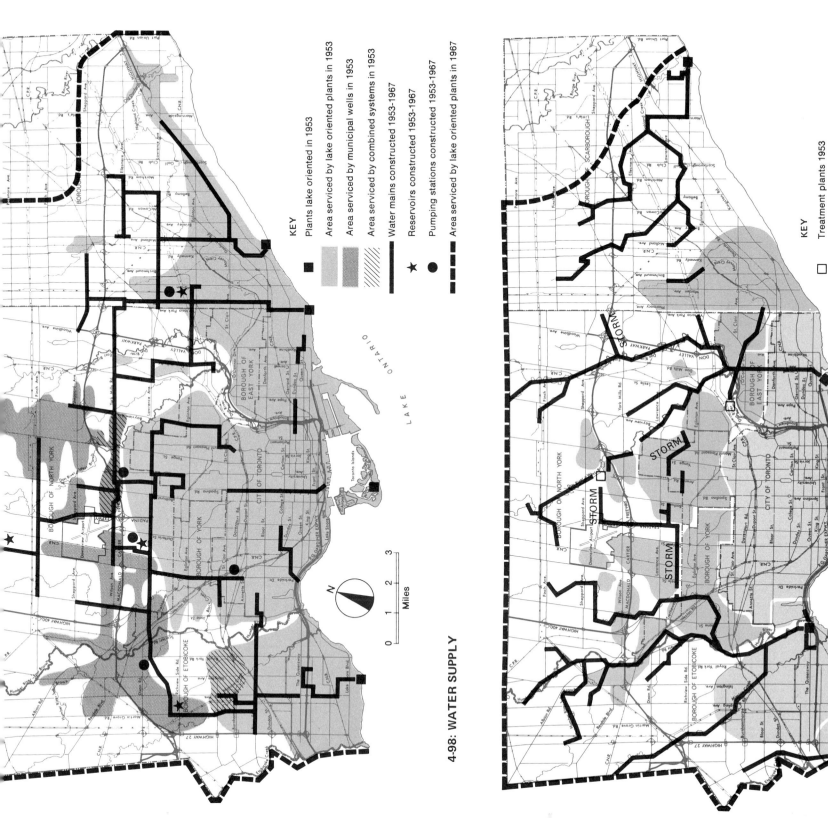

KEY

Plants lake oriented in 1953

Area serviced by lake oriented plants in 1953

Area serviced by municipal wells in 1953

Area serviced by combined systems in 1953

Water mains constructed 1953-1967

Reservoirs constructed 1953-1967

Pumping stations constructed 1953-1967

Area serviced by lake oriented plants in 1967

N

0 1 2 3 Miles

4-98: WATER SUPPLY

KEY

Treatment plants 1953

Area serviced by lake oriented plants in 1953

Area serviced by upstream plants in 1953

Trunk sewers constructed 1953-1967

Treatment plants enlarged or constructed 1953-1967

Area serviced by lake oriented plants in 1967

N

0 1 2 3 Miles

4-99: WATER POLLUTION CONTROL

Key
1. Parliament Buildings
2. East Block—Parliament Buildings
3. New Ontario Government Buildings
4. Royal Ontario Museum
5. McLaughlin Planetarium
6. Varsity Stadium
7. Queen's Park
   Black line defines general area of University campus.

4-100: The University of Toronto downtown campus and the Ontario Government buildings area

4-101: The University of Toronto and the Ontario Government buildings area, viewed from the east

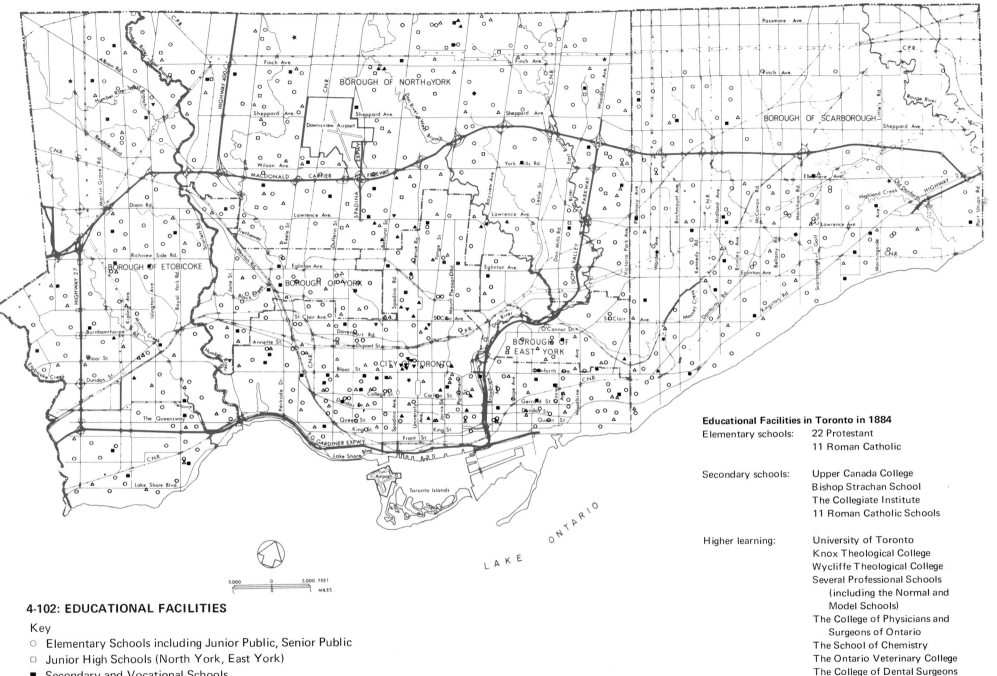

Educational Facilities in Toronto in 1884

Elementary schools: 22 Protestant
11 Roman Catholic

Secondary schools: Upper Canada College
Bishop Strachan School
The Collegiate Institute
11 Roman Catholic Schools

Higher learning: University of Toronto
Knox Theological College
Wycliffe Theological College
Several Professional Schools
(including the Normal and
Model Schools)
The College of Physicians and
Surgeons of Ontario
The School of Chemistry
The Ontario Veterinary College
The College of Dental Surgeons
The School of Dentistry
The School of Practical Science
The Toronto School of Medicine
Trinity Medical School
Osgoode Hall

4-102: EDUCATIONAL FACILITIES

Key

○ Elementary Schools including Junior Public, Senior Public

□ Junior High Schools (North York, East York)

■ Secondary and Vocational Schools

▲ Private Schools (including Jewish Schools and
Special Schools)

△ Schools of Metro Separate School Board

★ Community Colleges and Universities

7. SUMMARY OF LAND USES

Table 4-103 is essentially an inventory of the land uses of the Toronto area and, as such, is a valuable supplement to the general land use map. It is included at this point to illustrate how much land is used for various purposes and how various areas of the city differ from each other in terms of their land uses. The areas used are the Planning Districts that the Metropolitan Toronto Planning Board established as bases for much of its work (see Map 4-46, page 66).

Focal points

— The proportions of the various land uses in the Toronto area; the importance of the various land uses compared to the areas they cover

— Variations in land use in the planning districts; the balance of land uses in each Planning District

— Contrasts in land use distribution among the central area, the suburbs, and the edges of the urban complex

4-103: EXISTING LAND USES BY PLANNING DISTRICT 1966

Planning District	Residential		Industrial		Commercial		Open Space		Institutional		Transportation and Utilities		Vacant and Agricultural		Total Land Area	
	Acres	% of Total	Acres	% of Total	Acres	% of Total	Acres	% of Total	Acres	% of Total	Acres	% of Total	Acres	% of Total	Acres	% of Total
1	1,219	17.2	1,380	19.4	883	12.4	1,070	15.1	800	11.3	1,249	17.6	498	7.0	7,099	100.0%
2	3,616	58.6	420	6.8	485	7.9	892	14.4	305	4.9	364	5.9	93	1.5	6,175	
3	5,479	50.4	1,718	15.8	620	5.7	1,213	11.1	561	5.2	728	6.7	550	5.1	10,869	
4	6,513	64.3	452	4.1	448	4.4	1,317	13.0	659	6.5	413	4.1	334	3.3	10,136	
5	4,019	42.5	854	9.0	192	2.0	1,882	19.9	330	3.5	540	5.7	1,651	17.4	9,468	
6	4,643	60.7	433	5.7	447	5.9	960	12.6	402	5.2	545	7.1	214	2.8	7,644	
7	1,777	42.9	878	21.2	170	4.1	184	4.5	428	10.3	401	9.7	303	7.3	4,141	
8	7,844	49.0	925	5.8	452	2.8	2,153	13.4	615	3.8	1,410	8.8	2,619	16.4	16,018	
9	1,956	18.1	1,224	11.3	171	1.6	2,327	21.5	242	2.2	819	7.7	4,069	37.6	10,808	
10	2,964	23.3	1,279	10.0	182	1.4	1,537	12.1	463	3.6	1,666	13.1	4,696	36.5	12,737	
11	5,506	53.5	137	1.3	319	3.1	1,832	17.8	642	6.2	578	5.6	1,271	12.5	10,285	
12	997	23.2	3	.1	16	.4	473	11.0	69	1.6	333	7.8	2,402	55.9	4,293	
13	6,334	45.7	1,440	10.4	526	3.8	1,342	9.7	678	4.9	1,045	7.5	2,495	18.0	13,860	
14	2,657	55.5	51	1.1	176	3.7	786	16.4	286	6.0	124	2.6	703	14.7	4,783	
15	1,648	24.2	152	2.2	143	2.1	1,469	21.6	159	2.3	386	5.7	2,856	41.9	6,813	
16	1,760	9.1	500	2.7	165	.8	2,070	10.7	119	.6	1,341	6.6	13,396	69.4	19,351	
Metropolitan Toronto	58,932	38.2%	11,846	7.7%	5,395	3.5%	21,507	13.9%	6,758	4.4%	11,942	7.7%	38,100	29.6%	154,480	100.0%
17	2,843	13.0	1,161	5.3	139	.7	1,555	7.1	211	1.0	695	3.2	15,185	69.7	21,789	
18	5,181	9.7	1,761	3.3	400	.8	3,656	6.9	482	9.1	6,098	11.8	35,638	67.0	53,216	
19	1,008	1.9	139	.3	148	.3	7,913	14.7	99	.2	960	1.8	41,883	80.8	52,150	
20	4,135	6.8	1,319	2.2	282	.5	3,649	5.7	608	1.0	1,922	3.2	48,977	80.5	60,892	
21	1,800	4.2	135	.3	118	.3	1,836	4.3	113	.2	579	1.4	38,219	89.3	42,800	
22	792	1.5	347	.7	32	.1	3,431	6.6	41	.1	941	1.8	46,136	89.2	51,720	
23	2,698	11.2	333	1.4	92	.4	3,003	12.6	232	1.0	1,201	5.0	16,531	68.6	24,090	
Fringe Area	18,457	6.0%	5,195	1.7%	1,211	0.4%	25,043	8.2%	1,786	0.6%	12,396	4.0%	242,569	79.2%	306,657	100.0%
Metropolitan Toronto Planning Area	77,389	16.8%	17,041	3.7%	6,606	1.4%	46,550	10.1%	8,544	1.9%	24,338	5.3%	280,669	60.8%	461,137	100.0%

Source: Metropolitan Toronto Planning Board

8. A STUDY OF PART OF THE RURAL-URBAN FRINGE

Around the average city there is a zone of transition or change between urban land uses and the area that is devoted to agriculture. This zone is commonly referred to as the *rural-urban fringe*. While it is easy to recognize the obvious points of contact between the urban and rural uses, it is extremely difficult to indicate precisely the boundaries of a rural-urban fringe.

Only a small part of Toronto's fringe has been selected for study here and the problem of determining the extent of the fringe as a whole is not our concern. What follows is really a sample study—a collection of materials that reveal many of the most prominent features of a rural-urban fringe.

Focal points
- The general appearance of a rural-urban fringe
- The classifying of raw land use data into general categories; the creation of a general land use map
- The impact of an expanding city on a rural area: changes, conflicts and contrasts
- The particular problems of a rural-urban fringe
- Planning for future development in the fringe area

4-104: Views of the Rural-Urban Fringe

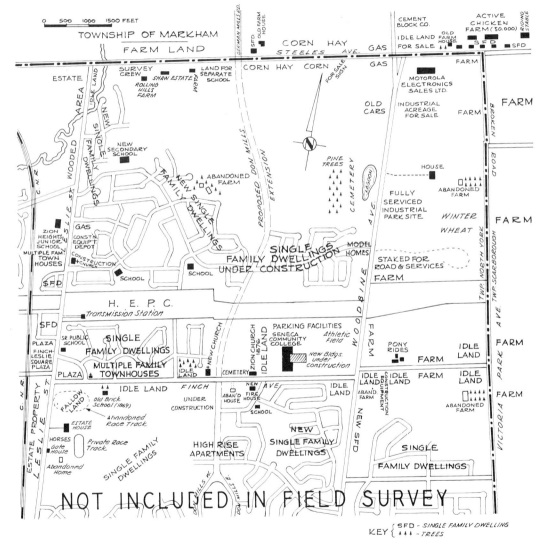

Map labels (clockwise / by area):

TOWNSHIP OF MARKHAM
FARM LAND

0 500 1000 1500 FEET

CORN HAY
STEELES AVE. GAS

CEMENT BLOCK CO.
IDLE LAND FOR SALE
OLD FARM HOUSE
SFD
SFD

ACTIVE CHICKEN FARM (50,000)
RIDING STABLE

SFD OLD FARM HOUSE
ESTATE
SURVEY CREW
SHAW ESTATE
ROLLING HILLS FARM
LAND FOR SEPARATE SCHOOL
CORN HAY CORN
FOR SALE SIGN
GAS
MOTOROLA ELECTRONICS SALES LTD.
FARM

WOODED AREA
IDLE LAND
NEW SINGLE FAMILY DWELLINGS
OLD CARS
INDUSTRIAL ACREAGE FOR SALE
FARM
BROKEN ROAD
FARM

NEW SECONDARY SCHOOL
PROPOSED DON MILLS EXTENSION
PINE TREES
CEMETERY
HOUSE
ABANDONED FARM

ABANDONED FARM
LAGOON
FULLY SERVICED INDUSTRIAL PARK SITE
WINTER WHEAT
FARM

ZION HEIGHTS JUNIOR SCHOOL
GAS
CONSTN. EQUIPT. DEPOT
SINGLE FAMILY DWELLINGS UNDER CONSTRUCTION
MODEL HOMES
STAKED FOR ROAD & SERVICES
FARM

MULTIPLE FAM. TOWN HOUSES
CONSTRUCTION + CHURCH
SCHOOL
SCHOOL

SFD
H.E.P.C. Transmission Station

SFD
PLAZA
FINCH-LESLIE SQUARE PLAZA
SR. PUBLIC SCHOOL
SINGLE FAMILY DWELLINGS
MULTIPLE FAMILY TOWNHOUSES
NEW CHURCH
PARKING FACILITIES
SENECA COMMUNITY COLLEGE
Athletic Field
ZION CHURCH 1876
IDLE LAND
New Bldgs. under construction
PONY RIDES
IDLE LAND
FARM
IDLE LAND

PLAZA
IDLE LAND
FALLOW LAND
Old Brick School (1869)
FINCH AVE.
UNDER CONSTRUCTION
CEMETERY
NEW FIRE HOUSE
SCHOOL
IDLE LAND
IDLE LAND
CONSTRUCTION EQUIPMENT
IDLE LAND
FARM
IDLE LAND
ABAN'D FARM
ABANDONED FARM

ESTATE PROPERTY
LESLIE ST.
CNR
ESTATE HOUSE
Abandoned Race Track
Abandoned Home
HORSES
Gate House
Private Race Track
SINGLE FAMILY DWELLINGS
HIGH RISE APARTMENTS
NEW SINGLE FAMILY DWELLINGS
NEW SFD
SINGLE FAMILY DWELLINGS

NOT INCLUDED IN FIELD SURVEY

KEY { SFD – SINGLE FAMILY DWELLING
♦♦♦ – TREES

4-105: RURAL-URBAN FRINGE AREA: LAND USE

4-106: The Rural-Urban Fringe area

96

9. CONSTRUCTION

Because it is an activity that results from developments in every sector of urban life, construction can reflect strongly a city's growth and prosperity.

Here and on several other pages in this book are materials that reveal certain aspects of construction in Toronto and show the relative importance of the city as a centre in which construction activities are concentrated.

4-107

4-108: VALUE OF BUILDING PERMITS ISSUED, 1968 (IN DOLLARS)

	Residential	Industrial	Commercial	Institutional	Total
Metropolitan Toronto	379,485,000	79,794,000	110,772,000	160,400,000	730,451,000
Metropolitan Montreal	295,716,000	71,128,000	77,159,000	107,300,000	551,303,000
Ontario	—	—	—	—	2,088,600,000
Quebec	—	—	—	—	1,066,100,000
Canada	—	—	—	—	4,700,200,000

Source: Dominion Bureau of Statistics

10. CITY STRUCTURE

In the introduction to Section IV we stated that the section contains much about the structure of Toronto and we defined structure as the arrangement and shapes of the various parts of a city and the general shape of the city as a whole.

Are basic patterns of structure repeated from city to city? Do all cities originate and develop in the same general way? These and other important questions about city structure are the concerns of many urban scholars who seek the answers to them with a view to gaining a deeper understanding of the city and improving the quality of urban life.

Three theoretical explanations of city structure have commanded considerable attention for many years. The basic ideas of each are presented in the outlines that follow.

1. The Concentric Zone Theory of E. W. Burgess (Diagram 4-109)

According to Burgess a city takes the form of five concentric zones.

Zone 1. The Central Business District. At the centre of a city lies its focus of commercial, social and civic life, and transportation. In large cities this area becomes subdivided into specialized districts: retail, office and financial. Around the centre lies the wholesale area with its markets and warehouses and other storage facilities.

Zone 2. The Zone of Transition. Around the Central Business District is a zone of residential deterioration. Businesses and light industry have encroached upon residential areas. Here are to be found a city's worst and most widespread slums.

Zone 3. The Zone of Independent Working-men's Homes. Many of the people who live in this zone are people who have moved out of Zone 2. Second generation immigrants often live in this zone.

Zone 4. The Zone of Better Residences. This is the zone in which the typical middle class person lives. Here are the homes of small business owners, professionals, clerks, and salesmen. Single-family dwellings become replaced by apartment buildings. Commercial sub-centres develop at strategic points.

Zone 5. The Commuters' Zone. Beyond the city itself lies a ring of small cities and towns. Fairly high quality residential areas develop along major transportation routes. Most of the residents work in the Central Business District.

(It is interesting to note that many other elements making up a city, not just the ones Burgess mentions, tend to form a basically concentric pattern as well.)

2. The Sector Theory of
Homer Hoyt (Diagram 4-110)
The sector theory deals only with residential land. Residential areas, Hoyt claims, tend to be arranged in wedges or *sectors* that radiate out from the city centre along major transportation lines.

Hoyt felt that housing rent was a reliable indication in determining the structure of residential areas. Areas of approximately the same rent form sectors, not concentric rings. For example, high rent areas in the city tend to be located in one or more sectors. Intermediate rent areas tend to adjoin the high rent areas and to be located in the same sectors as the high rent areas. Low rent areas occupy other sectors from the centre out to the edge. As the city expands, the various rent areas tend to migrate outward, following their respective sectors.

3. The Multiple Nuclei Concept of
Chauncy Harris and Edward L.
Ullman (Diagram 4-111)
In this concept, Harris and Ullman have combined features of the concentric zone and sector theories and added some ideas of their own. They suggest that the land use patterns of a city typically form around several distinct and separate centres or nuclei, not around one centre as claimed by both Burgess and Hoyt. Some cities *originate* around several nuclei and others around just one, but as any city grows it stimulates the development of more nuclei. For example, an industry moves out of an older area of the city to establish a modern plant beyond the edges of the city. That new plant can become the nucleus for new urban development.

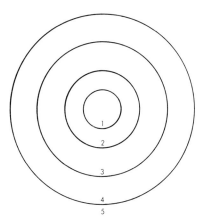

4-109: CONCENTRIC ZONE THEORY

Key

(1) The Central Business District; (2) Zone in Transition; (3) Zone of Independent Working-men's Homes; (4) Zone of Better Residences; (5) Commuters' Zone

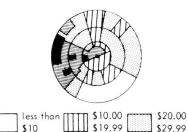

less than $10	$10.00 $19.99	$20.00 $29.99

$30.00 $49.99	$50 or more

4-110: SECTOR THEORY

These figures are based on U.S. Federal Housing Administration figures for 1939.

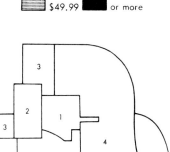

4-111: MULTIPLE NUCLEI THEORY

Key

(1) Central Business District; (2) Wholesale Light Manufacturing; (3) Low Class Residential; (4) Medium Class Residential; (5) High Class Residential; (6) Heavy Manufacturing; (7) Outlying Business District; (8) Residential Suburb; (9) Industrial Suburb

Focal points

— The ways in which Toronto's structure agrees with and differs from the three theories, as evidenced by the basic patterns revealed by the materials listed below or any other materials that may be applicable.

Source: *The American City*, by Raymond E. Murphy. © 1966 by McGraw-Hill, Inc. Used with permission of McGraw-Hill Book Company

SECTION 5 METROPOLITAN TORONTO

Toronto has become one of the largest metropolitan centres in North America. Moreover, it is the principal nucleus of a large urban region that curves around the west end of Lake Ontario and is commonly referred to as *The Golden Horseshoe*. The problems of administering a populous, sprawling city located in such a geographic situation are staggering. Toronto's response to the situation was to establish a system of metropolitan government.

This section deals with the meaning of *metropolitanism* in general and provides materials that illustrate the nature of Toronto's metropolitan government—a system that has gained international attention.

Focal points
— The meaning of metropolitanism
— The reasons for the establishment of a metropolitan government in the Toronto area
— Problems resulting from the incorporation of several municipalities into one federation
— The future of metropolitan government in the Toronto area

The Gras Hypothesis
One interesting attempt to explain the rise of a town or small city to metropolitan status was made some years ago by Professor N. S. B. Gras.* Gras notes four phases that most of the large centres of the world have gone through.

Phase 1. The town creates a well-organized trading or marketing system for itself and its hinterland. In this phase, the town becomes the focus for the trade of the surrounding area. Business establishments in the town buy goods from the merchants of the town and the hinterland, and store, transport and sell these goods to consumers in the town and the hinterland. Gradually, the town becomes the most important trading centre of the region. When this stage is reached the foundation of a metropolitan economy has been laid.

Phase 2. An increase in the development of manufactures, either in the city or its

---

* Gras, N. S. B., *An Introduction to Economic History,* Harper and Brothers Publishers, 1922

hinterland. To be a metropolis, a city must possess a great variety of commodities—a full store of all goods that are available and in demand. These goods may be obtained by trade or produced in the marketing centre itself and its surrounding area by various manufacturing enterprises. The existence of a large demand right in the city itself is, of course, a major attraction for industries.

Phase 3. The development of transportation. As most cities and their regions develop their manufactures, improvements in transportation are made that further the development of trade. Within the city itself measures are taken to reduce congestion and stimulate efficient traffic flow. Communications between the city and its hinterland are improved also. At this stage, while metropolitan status has not yet been reached, the city's economy and that of its hinterland is well developed or mature.

Phase 4. The construction of a well-developed financial system. From its beginning, of course, a city must develop financial resources—banks, exchanges, etc.—to promote trade. But the full measure of growth in a city's financial function comes when that function becomes large and important enough to influence strongly and even to direct business operations not only within the hinterland but beyond it as well. When the economy has reached this stage, it may be said to be a metropolitan economy.

The Establishment of a Metropolitan Government in Toronto
The years immediately following the Second World War marked the beginning of a period of population growth unprecedented in the history of the Toronto area. During the years 1945-1956, in what is today Metropolitan Toronto, the population increased by over 400,000—more people than the present total population of the city of Calgary. All of that growth occurred in the 12 suburban municipalities surrounding the City of Toronto; the population of the City itself remained almost static. This sudden, huge jump in population created serious problems.

The primary responsibility of every municipality is to provide a wide range of public

services to its inhabitants. These services are paid for by local taxation. Large and rapid increases in population lead to rising costs in providing services and these costs, in turn, lead to higher and higher taxes. By the early 1950's, the suburban municipalities faced major financial difficulties in attempting to meet the rapidly rising demand for services.

The situation was aggravated by the geographical division of the suburban area into 12 municipalities of greatly varying sizes. Some had no direct physical access to Lake Ontario—the principal source of water supply and the final outlet for sanitary and storm sewage. In North York, for example, water supplied from wells, and sewage treatment by septic tanks or small upstream plants soon proved inadequate. Similarly, some of the municipalities were far better situated than others with respect to highway and railway facilities, recreational areas and rivers.

As the separate municipalities grew it became evident that their relationships with each other were, of necessity, becoming closer and that satisfactory inter-municipal arrangements for the provision of services were growing more and more important.

Several solutions to the local government crisis were offered and discussed before the Ontario Municipal Board. The City of Toronto, for example, proposed amalgamation with the nine inner suburbs and the urbanized parts of the three large townships of Etobicoke, North York and Scarborough. Almost all of the suburban municipalities, anxious to preserve a system of strong local governments in the area, opposed the idea. Several of them, however, favoured the formation of an area in which the responsibility of providing services was to be a joint effort.

After holding extensive hearings and carefully considering the evidence submitted by the municipalities concerned, the Ontario Municipal Board, on January 20, 1953, handed down a decision recommending the establishment of a metropolitan system of government for the City of Toronto and the 12 suburban municipalities around it. The following passage is from the Board's historic report:

"The central question is whether the continued existence of local municipal govern-

ments, carrying out necessary and important functions of a local nature, is, after all, completely inconsistent with the concurrent existence of a senior metropolitan government equipped with adequate powers and resources to deal with area-wide problems. It is the opinion of the board that the most promising avenue of approach to a solution of this question is clearly indicated in the political history of our own nation, and that many of the fundamental principles so wisely applied in the federation of the British North American Provinces can be profitably adapted in the organization of a suitable form of local government in this area. The board cannot attempt any exposition of the political theory which found expression in the British North America Act of 1867, nor will it refer to the striking similarity between the position of the provinces prior to Confederation and that of the municipalities in the Toronto area eighty-five years later. It is sufficient to point out that in every true federation there is a recognition of the need for a dual system of government, an acceptance of the idea that the establishment of a strong central authority is the best method of dealing with vital problems affecting the entire area, and a conviction that the retention of local governments for local purposes is not only desirable but necessary.

"If the principle of federation is to be applied in the organization of a metropolitan government, it is immediately obvious that a sound answer must be found to the vital question of the division of powers between the local governments and the central authority and that a matter of almost equal importance is the constitution and organization of the central or metropolitan authority.

"Before submitting its proposals with respect to the distribution of powers and responsibilities, the board feels that an explanation should be given of the general principles which have been followed in making a selection. In the first place, the board has carefully avoided any unnecessary reduction of the existing powers of the local authorities with the object of preserving the greatest possible degree of local autonomy. In the opinion of the board this is particularly important during the critical initial period of adjustment which is bound to follow the inauguration of the new system regardless of its merits. A practical consideration is the need to avoid drastic and sweeping changes in the existing administrative organization of the various municipalities. Important changes will certainly be required, but everything possible should be done to insure an orderly transition. The board has, for these reasons, intentionally left with the local governments certain important matters which might quite logically be included within the sphere of operations of the central authority, and which may well be transferred to it at a later stage without serious objection. It is not by any means the view of the board that the central authority should eventually take over all of the important functions now performed by the local councils and their local boards. The board is convinced that the local governments will always have a vital role in the general scheme of metropolitan government. This should not prevent the gradual and orderly transfer to the central authority of certain additional powers which may now be described as desirable but not immediately essential. With respect to these, it is the opinion of the board that their transfer should await the gradual development of public opinion after the new system has been placed

in operation. The board wishes to emphasize at this point the fact that one of the great virtues of any federal scheme is its flexibility and the comparative ease with which it can be adapted to changed conditions and the realities of a particular situation. This is especially true in the case of municipalities created by the legislature and exercising delegated powers only. They are not in the position of sovereign states entering a federation on a contractual basis and the scheme of federation now proposed will not be comparable to a rigid written constitution to be amended only by mutual consent. Necessary changes can and will be made as the need arises by the act of the legislature which is at all times the only source of the powers which are being discussed. It should not be forgotten, moreover, that the great body of important and somewhat complicated legislation controlling the operation of Ontario municipalities has been the result of a long evolutionary process and most of the important changes have been made in response to the requests of the municipalities themselves.

"While the board has thus recognized the continuing need for strong local governments, it has not hesitated to assign to the central authority definite responsibility for the functions and services considered vitally

necessary to the continued growth and development of the entire area as an urban community. In particular it is considered essential that the central metropolitan government should have jurisdiction over certain physical and other services which must be provided at all costs in the housing of the present and future population ultimately responsible for the prosperity of the area. In the same class are the municipal services required to supplement the outstanding advantages of the area as a centre of industry and commerce. The board is convinced that the only way in which services of this type can be provided when and where they are needed is to place them under the jurisdiction of the central authority and to make the combined resources of the entire area available to finance them . . ."*

The Government of Ontario adopted the Municipality of Metropolitan Toronto Act (Bill 80). The newly formed Metropolitan Toronto Council assumed jurisdiction over an area of 240 square miles consisting of the City of Toronto and its 12 suburbs on January 1, 1954. Frederick G. Gardiner was the Council's first Chairman.

The Metropolitan Corporation made some remarkable progress in its first decade. It gained

widespread support for the general concept of metropolitan government in Toronto and it resolved the services crisis. There were, however, some serious basic problems in the experiment. Differences in financial strength continued to plague the member municipalities. Also, there developed a growing concern about representation on Metropolitan Council. In 1963 the Ontario Government appointed a Royal Commission on Metropolitan Toronto and in June that Commission handed down a report recommending consolidation of the area into four cities. The Metropolitan Corporation was to assume many new responsibilities and powers and to undertake a major overhaul of the metropolitan school system. In May 1966 the Ontario Government adopted an act (Bill 81) which incorporated many of the Royal Commission's recommendations. The most important feature of the reorganization was the reduction of the number of municipalities from 13 to 6—a modification of the Royal Commission's proposal regarding administrative structure.

---

*Source: The Ontario Municipal Board, Decisions and Recommendations of the Board, Dated January 20, 1953

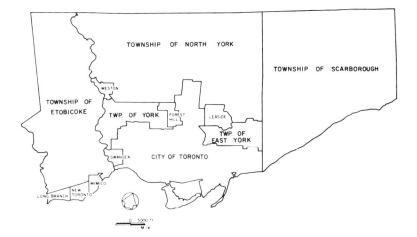

5-1: THE MUNICIPALITY OF METROPOLITAN TORONTO, 1953

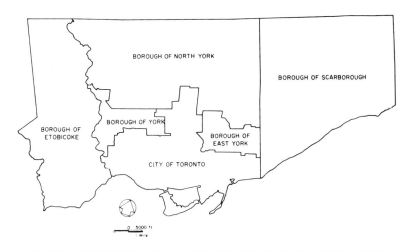

5-2: THE MUNICIPALITY OF METROPOLITAN TORONTO, 1967

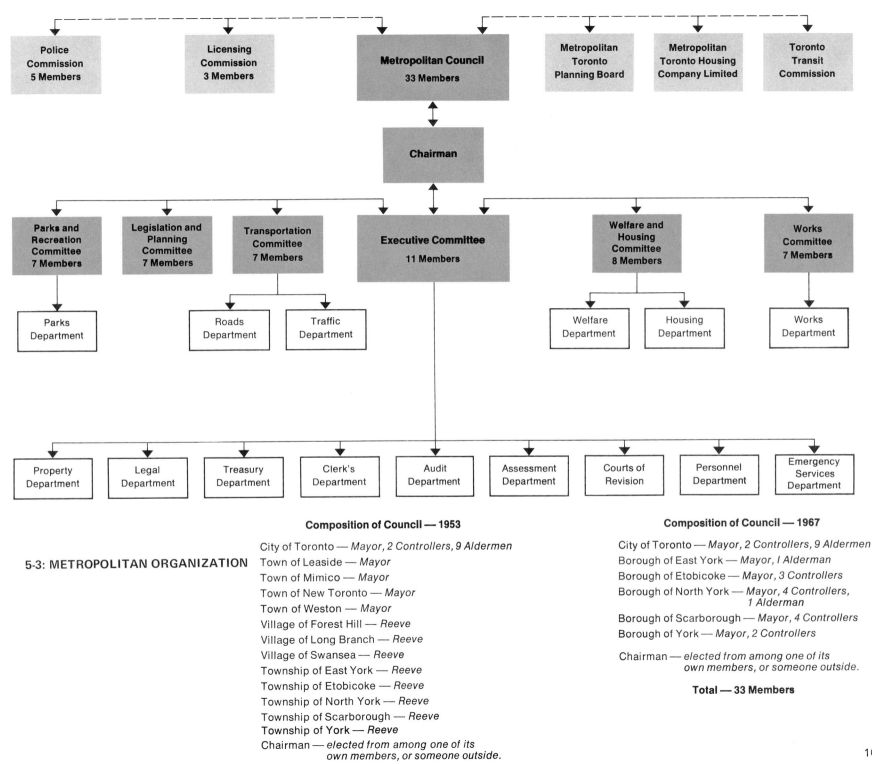

Police Commission 5 Members	Licensing Commission 3 Members	**Metropolitan Council** 33 Members	Metropolitan Toronto Planning Board	Metropolitan Toronto Housing Company Limited	Toronto Transit Commission

Chairman

Parks and Recreation Committee 7 Members

Legislation and Planning Committee 7 Members

Transportation Committee 7 Members

Executive Committee 11 Members

Welfare and Housing Committee 8 Members

Works Committee 7 Members

Parks Department

Roads Department — Traffic Department

Welfare Department — Housing Department

Works Department

Property Department | Legal Department | Treasury Department | Clerk's Department | Audit Department | Assessment Department | Courts of Revision | Personnel Department | Emergency Services Department

5-3: METROPOLITAN ORGANIZATION

Composition of Council — 1953

City of Toronto — *Mayor, 2 Controllers, 9 Aldermen*
Town of Leaside — *Mayor*
Town of Mimico — *Mayor*
Town of New Toronto — *Mayor*
Town of Weston — *Mayor*
Village of Forest Hill — *Reeve*
Village of Long Branch — *Reeve*
Village of Swansea — *Reeve*
Township of East York — *Reeve*
Township of Etobicoke — *Reeve*
Township of North York — *Reeve*
Township of Scarborough — *Reeve*
Township of York — *Reeve*
Chairman — *elected from among one of its own members, or someone outside.*

Total — 25 Members

Composition of Council — 1967

City of Toronto — *Mayor, 2 Controllers, 9 Aldermen*
Borough of East York — *Mayor, I Alderman*
Borough of Etobicoke — *Mayor, 3 Controllers*
Borough of North York — *Mayor, 4 Controllers, 1 Alderman*
Borough of Scarborough — *Mayor, 4 Controllers*
Borough of York — *Mayor, 2 Controllers*

Chairman — *elected from among one of its own members, or someone outside.*

Total — 33 Members

5-4: RESPONSIBILITIES OF THE METROPOLITAN GOVERNMENT

M — Metropolitan Toronto
A — Area Municipalities

Finance and taxation
Assessment of property	M	
Courts of revision	M	A
Taxation of property		A
Debenture borrowing	M	
Local improvement charges		A

Planning
Official plans	M	A
Subdivision approval	M	A
Zoning		A

Recreation and community services
Regional parks	M	
Local parks		A
Recreation programs		A
Community centres and arenas		A
Municipal golf courses	M	
Municipal zoo	M	
Regional libraries	M	
Local libraries	M	A

Road construction and maintenance
Expressways	M	
Arterial roads	M	
Local roads		A
Bridges and grade separations	M	A
Snow removal	M	A
Street cleaning	M	A
Sidewalks		A

Traffic control
Traffic regulations	M	A
Cross-walks	M	A
Traffic lights	M	
Street lighting		A
Pavement markings	M	A

Public transit
Toronto Transit Commission	M	

Water supply
Purification, pumping and trunk distribution system	M	
Local distribution		A
Collection of water bills		A

Sewage disposal
Sanitary trunk system and disposal plants	M	
Connecting systems		A
Storm drainage	M	A

Garbage collection and disposal
Collection		A
Disposal sites	M	

Air pollution
Air pollution control	M	

Public education
Operation of public school system		A
School sites, attendance areas and building programs	M	
Operating costs	M	
Capital costs	M	

Housing
Elderly persons housing	M	
Low rental family housing	M	
Moderate rental family housing	M	A

Welfare
Welfare assistance	M	
Hospitalization of indigents	M	
Assistance to Children's Aid Societies	M	
Homes for the aged	M	
Other services	M	

Health
Public health services		A
Chronic and convalescent hospital	M	
Hospital grants		A
Ambulance services	M	

Police and fire protection
Police	M	
Fire		A

Administration of justice
Magistrates' courts	M	
Court house and jail	M	
Juvenile and family court	M	
Coroner's office	M	
Registry and land titles offices	M	

Licensing and inspection
Business licensing	M	
Dog licensing and pound		A
Marriage licenses		A
Building by-laws		A

Civil defence
Emergency Measures	M	

Other municipal services
Collection of fines	M	A
Collection of vital statistics		A
Distribution of hydro electric power		A
Grants to cultural organizations	M	A
Harbour		A
Island airport		A
Municipal parking lots		A
Preparation of voters' lists and administration of civic elections		A
Redevelopment	M	A

5-5: GROSS EXPENDITURES* OF THE MUNICIPALITY OF METROPOLITAN TORONTO FOR THE YEAR ENDED DECEMBER 31, 1968

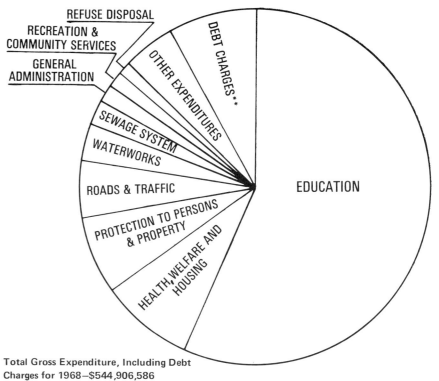

Total Gross Expenditure, Including Debt Charges for 1968—$544,906,586

* *Gross Expenditures* are the amounts of money spent by the municipality without taking into account revenue of any kind.

** *Debt Charges* are the annual costs (principal and interest) of paying back the money that the municipality borrowed to finance certain major projects.

Source: The Municipality of Metropolitan Toronto, Annual Report of the Commissioner of Finance, 1968

SECTION 6 TORONTO LIFE

It is almost impossible to describe city life accurately and completely. Nevertheless, one can form strong impressions of what it is like to live in Toronto or to visit Toronto through an examination of many of the materials in this book, especially those in this section which deal directly with the subject of life quality.

Focal points
- Toronto as a place in which to live
- Toronto as a place to visit
- The availability and accessibility of leisure-time facilities
- Evidence that there are areas within Toronto each of which has a life-style or personality that makes it truly distinctive
- Trends in Toronto life; the changing image of the city

6-1: BIG CITY! GROWING UP WITH TORONTO

by Peter Gzowski

. . . I can remember—not remember reading about, but *remember*—a Toronto when it was illegal to sell liquor by the glass, or to go to a movie on Sunday; when there was a law against sunbathing in the park, when the mayor made an outraged speech because the University of Toronto was showing a painting that exposed a woman's breast, and when the newspapers used to paint out the woman's navel in any photograph of a two-piece bathing suit. And now within the two-mile radius where I grew up there are bars and night clubs of every description: elegant, corny, gaudy and secret. Sunday is the biggest movie day of the week, and a big day, too, for live theatre and concerts, puppet shows and skating on the city hall plaza, hockey games and bowling tournaments and—perhaps especially—for the Victory Burlesque house, the old movie theatre across from St. Elizabeth of Hungary Church, which features (the burlesque house, not the church) amateur strip-tease contests where "you may see the girl next door." If I—to insert yet another personal note—wanted to see the girl next door, frankly, I think I'd go next door, but the new Toronto is a new Toronto for everyone, and the Victory thrives.

This is not to say we are having a giant, municipal orgy over here, all two million of us. Toronto the Good, as the city used to be called in a manner not intended as flattery, has scarcely become Toronto the Bad. At its core, there are still the blue-haired ladies and the traditions of Scottish propriety that shaped so much of its early moral thinking. It's still impossible to buy a drink after one o'clock in the morning. Although the parks are pleasant places, lovers seldom kiss there—and the law against taking your shirt off to enjoy the sun was repealed only in 1966.

The easy way out here, in trying to explain my affection for Toronto, would be to go through the magazine-writer's contrast routine

(Munich is a city of contrasts . . . India is a country of paradox . . . South America is a continent on the horns of a dilemma, and so on). But the point about Toronto, I think, is a subtler one. Toronto was founded by British and Scots in the eighteenth century; it grew fitfully—the fits triggered usually by the pressures of wars and economics—until the middle of the twentieth century, when it was still primarily a big *town,* predominantly British. (One of the big annual entertainments was the Orangemen's Parade.) And then it exploded. What had first been a small Irish ghetto in the lower western half of the city, and then a slightly bigger Jewish ghetto, made up mostly of workers for the garment centre, and then had begun to empty as the second-generation Jews moved their families uptown and into the middle classes, was suddenly filled with Italians. Quickly, they over-ran the ghetto's edges west and north. Now, Toronto has more than a quarter of a million Italians—one of the biggest Italian cities in the world outside New York—and Italian movies and espresso houses and newspapers too; you can, if you want, live your entire life in Toronto speaking only Italian.

The ghetto, as such, ceased to exist. All over the city the new citizens spread out—Portuguese, Germans, Chinese, Americans, Hungarians, Austrians, Estonians . . . a list as long as the United Nations. They had been coming before, immigrants; now they were coming by the thousands, and, speaking their strange languages and reading their pictureless newspapers, they were becoming instant Torontonians. Where they had been absorbed, they began to absorb—or at least to influence. And with them came the bright young men and women from the Canadian prairies and the Maritime provinces, from the small towns to the big one. Toronto is the industrial centre of Canada. The St. Lawrence Seaway has opened

its port on Lake Ontario to the world's seas. Dominion-wide railroads slash across its waterfront. Brand new factories leapfrog out into its exurbs—new ones every day, it seems to us residents, attracting new residential settlements, new schools, new shopping plazas. Its stock exchange trades more shares than any other in the world. It is the political centre of the province, and its metropolitan system of government is a delicate balance between the suburbs and the nucleus city that has been studied by other growing municipalities all over the world. It is also the centre of publishing, broadcasting and the arts in English-speaking Canada. A second university, York, has sprung up as the University of Toronto, where I was one of twelve thousand undergraduates in the middle-1950's, now finds its capacity of more than twenty-five thousand is not enough to meet the new demands. True, there is a hectic pace here, the pace of a big city growing bigger. And I know some people react against it. To some of us, though—as to those of us who work on Toronto's three highly competitive daily newspapers—the pace, the rat-race, only adds to the excitement. In trying to outdo each other with each edition, we serve the public better—and, with the added edge of competition, I think we have more fun.

Unlike the United States, Canada has never presumed to be a melting pot of nationalities. Nor has Toronto. And with the pull of its internal energy, Toronto is drawing more and more divergent new people every year. But in that divergency lies our growing identity—a mixed city, unlike any other place in the world. What has happened, in other words, is that the explosion has changed the big town into a big city. . . .

Reprinted with permission from *Ontario 67.* Courtesy of the Ontario Government Department of Trade and Development.

6-4

6-7

6-9

6-2

6-5

6-8

6-10

6-3

6-6

6-11

SUTTON PLACE

6-12

Upcoming Calendar

January

16 Toronto Symphony Charter Series

Andres Segovia Massey Hall 8:30

17 Toronto Maple Leafs vs. the Pittsburgh Penguins tonight at Maple Leaf Gardens. Game time: 8:00 pm

18 A program of comic opera by the St. Augustine Boys' Choir East York Library at 3:00 pm

19 The Ice Follies open tomorrow at Maple Leaf Gardens for the week

20 21 Toronto Symphony, Rafael Fruhbeck De Burgos cond. Huguette Tourangean mezzo soprano Massey Hall 8:30 (Series B/B1)

22 "A Man's A Man" until Saturday at Hart House performed by U of T Centre for the Study of Drama.

23 Folk Art Festival at Northern Seconday School 7:00 pm

24 "A Night with Robbie Burns" featuring Lex McLean and other Scottish stars plus Danny Dial and The Pacific Show Band at Massey Hall. Tickets 653-1127

25 Amateur Theatre 'The Telephone' and 'La Voix Humaine' at Scarborough College at 3:45 pm. Admission free

26 SPRING THAW '70 IS A NEW BAG.

Spring Thaw starts previews tomorrow at The Playhouse 8:30 pm Tickets 481-3378

27 28 Toronto Symphony (Series A) Kazuyoshi Akiyama Cond. Itzhak Perlman Violin Massey Hall 8:30

29 Toronto Calendar Magazine arrives today

Further on

Feb. 5 Jacqueline Du Pré and Daniel Barenboim at Massey Hall.

Feb. 6 Toronto International Boat Show opens

Feb. 9 Marcel Marceau at Burton Auditorium, York U

Reproduced by permission of *Toronto Calendar Magazine* from issue of December 19, 1969

6-13

6-14: WHAT THE PEOPLE SAY

A supervisor; former resident of the Maritimes; resident of Toronto for 14 years; bachelor; age 32

"The only thing I had ever heard about Toronto was my uncle's view. In 1944, while waiting for a connecting train at Union Station, he had stepped out onto Front Street and seen a stone wall. Having driven into Toronto, I took the first possible opportunity to see this stone wall. One look at the Royal York Hotel and I longed for the open fields and woods of home.

"Making friends with people at work is hampered by the fact that you may live in the west end and he in the east end.

"To get to any open areas of Ontario, a Toronto resident has the perpetual dread of facing that weekend traffic.

"I have generally found that a person born and raised in Toronto does not know Toronto. He does know every nook and cranny in his own block, the way to work and the way to Queen and Yonge for shopping. Some west end residents have never crossed the dividing line, anything east of Yonge Street is a foreign country.

"I have found that the hustle-bustle type of life in Toronto has become second nature to me. I returned home for a vacation recently, the first time in almost 10 years, and I was amazed at the slow, methodical, complacent attitude of the people. A next-door neighbour took his car to the garage to have an oil change, tune up and tires rotated, then drove to Halifax and back which he considered to be a two-day trip. On returning he took his car back to the garage for an oil change, tune up and tires rotated. The return trip to Halifax is approximately 200 miles on a Trans-Canada Highway. I've gone to Niagara Falls in the evening for coffee and never thought twice about it. The slow pace of life is sometimes nice for a vacation, but it was a relief to return to Toronto."

A waitress from Budapest, Hungary; married, no children; resident of Toronto for 3 years; former student of journalism (in Hungary); age 28

"I find living in Toronto not very much different from living in Budapest when I'm in the routine of day to day work. It's during my non-working time that I notice the big differences. I miss the many inexpensive year-round live theatre performances especially. Also, Budapest is a far better city for recreation: it has more swimming pools for one thing and you don't have to be a member to be able to use any of the many sports clubs. Another thing I miss is being able to have a drink, if I want, at any restaurant. And speaking of restaurants, why doesn't Toronto have more sidewalk cafes?

"I can remember very clearly that my first impression of Toronto was that it was very dirty. Toronto people just don't seem to bother to keep the city clean. And one sad thing about Toronto is that it seems to have missed the chance to do something attractive with its waterfront. The Island is beautiful (I love the signs that say "Please Walk on the Grass"), but the mainland shore is just plain ugly.

"I do like Kensington Market—it's interesting and charming. And the Don Valley Parkway gives wonderful views of some very glamorous high-rise areas of the city. As a matter of fact, the only times I feel that Toronto is a big city is when I'm travelling on an expressway and when I'm right downtown.

"As far as the people of Toronto are concerned, I disagree with the common opinion that they are not friendly—I find they are."

A senior citizen; widow; resident of a metro home for the aged; age 83

"Having lived in Toronto since 1906 I have seen many changes. Our city has grown so fast and beautiful with many improvements and interests from child welfare to senior citizens. We old folk are thankful for the foresight of our churches and city fathers in building such comfortable homes for us. When our families find we need more care and attention than they can give it is wonderful we can find a home with people our own age and interests. We have much in common and enjoy talking about our early days in Toronto. Most of us have grandchildren so we are never lost for a topic to talk about. I remember the long walk to the island ferry and the open street car, our churches that were always full on Sundays, Kew Beach where we had so many picnics and swam, then the long ride home in the street car. Above all we thank God for those who built homes for us to enjoy in our old age."

A teacher; bachelor living in midtown high-rise apartment; age 48

"The city of Toronto means to me what New York might represent to many Americans—a crystallization of the best and the worst that Canada as a whole possesses. Here, contained within a few concentrated miles of a congested downtown, are the finest and the drabbest of entertaineries, eateries, apartments, stores and people. People of all backgrounds, like the mixed architectures of incongruously adjacent buildings, come into greater or lesser contact on crowded sidewalks, in occasional parks, clean subways and WASPish concert halls. People, 2,000,000 strong, provide devotees for all tastes and anonymities amid numbers. Toronto offers, as well as the inevitable debris of an industrial centre, choices in life style that almost make the rat-race and sophistication seem exciting and worthwhile and with the coming of summer it is unquestionably the greatest place in the world to get away from."

An American business executive from Cleveland, Ohio; male; age 51

"For the out-of-town visitor, Toronto's accommodations and restaurant facilities compare favourably with the better offerings of northern United States cities. In recent years, restaurants specializing in a wide range of nationalistic dishes have provided a variety of delicious menus representative of the cosmopolitan, ethnic flavour of Toronto's 'new' population. These excellent facilities are an attraction to visitors and provide a comfortable atmosphere in which to relax during the course of business discussions.

"As a local population it would be difficult to identify cultural or social differences between Torontonians and northern Americans. As individuals, Torontonians are as much like some Americans as they are different from others; but, as a generality northern Americans and Torontonians have much in common. They speak the same language, they have essentially the same religious beliefs and attend the same types of places of worship, they have much the same business interests and follow the same business practices. They like the same type of sports and they drive the same automobiles."

A suburban Toronto housewife; 3 children; husband teaches in a central area school; age 32

"We own a reasonably priced home which is quite adequate in size, with a large garden. A comparable home in the city would be much more expensive.

"The area itself is quiet and clean and there is very little traffic and therefore not much danger where children are concerned. There are plenty of other children with whom mine can become acquainted.

"However, I do find some disadvantages in living here. Although the houses are neat, they tend to look alike both externally and internally. They are very close together which prevents any real privacy, and one tends to feel obliged to keep up the neat appearance of the property at all times.

"Although there are several large stores in the area, there isn't the wide selection of merchandise that is available in the downtown area. Also the good restaurants are all in the centre of the city.

"Transportation facilities are not really adequate if there is no car at one's disposal, and it is a long drive to a city job.

"The social activities of the housewives run on a somewhat superficial level, consisting for the most part of coffee groups, tupperware parties, and doing the weekly shopping together. If one were to become too involved in these types of things, it would be difficult to retain much individual privacy."

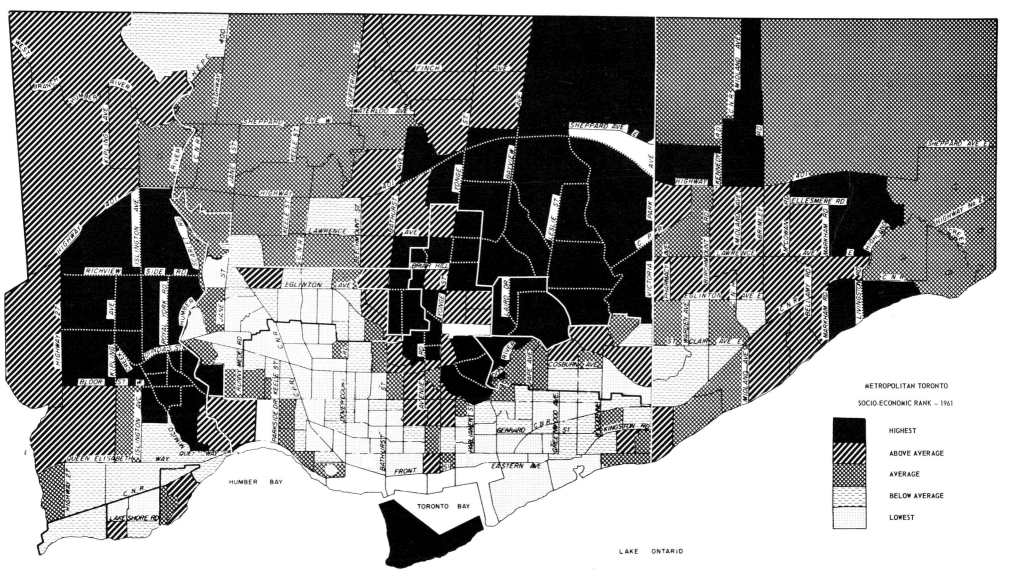

METROPOLITAN TORONTO

SOCIO-ECONOMIC RANK – 1961

HIGHEST

ABOVE AVERAGE

AVERAGE

BELOW AVERAGE

LOWEST

LAKE ONTARIO

6-15: SOCIO-ECONOMIC RANK, 1961

Socio-economic characteristics reflect a great many aspects of a city's people and their modes of life. This map brings into combination the factors of *income, occupation* and *education*. To arrive at their rankings, the Social Planning Council of Metropolitan Toronto calculated

1. the per cent of the male labour force with an annual wage and salary income $6,000 and over

2. the per cent of the male labour force in managerial, professional and technical occupations

3. the per cent of the total population not attending school, five years of age and over, who have attended university

The one-fifth with the highest scores are shown as Highest and the one-fifth with the lowest scores are shown as Lowest. The three-fifths between these extremes were then ranked Above Average, Average and Below Average.

6-16: SELECTED NON-WORKING TIME FACILITIES

Theatres
1 O'Keefe Centre
2 Royal Alexandra
3 St. Lawrence Centre
   & Town Hall
4 Playhouse Theatre
5 Toronto Workshop Theatre
6 Central Library Theatre
7 Colonnade Theatre
8 Theatre in the Dell
9 Theatre Passe Muraille
10 Global Village
11 Studio Lab Theatre
12 Victory Burlesque
13 Poor Alex
14 Hart House Theatre

Concert Halls
15 Eaton Auditorium
16 Edward Johnson Bldg.
17 Massey Hall

Sports Centres
18 Varsity Stadium
19 CNE Stadium
20 Hockey Hall of Fame
21 Maple Leaf Gardens
22 Stanley Park

Miscellaneous
23 Art Gallery of Ontario
24 Woodbine Racetrack
25 Greenwood Racetrack
26 The Zoo
27 Allan Gardens

28 Edwards Gardens
29 The CNE Grounds

Historical Sites
30 Old Fort York
31 Casa Loma
32 Mackenzie House
33 Pioneer Village
34 Todmorden Mills

Museums, etc.
35 Royal Ontario Museum
36 Marine Museum
37 McLaughlin Planetarium
38 Ontario Science Centre

Clubs
39 Cedarbrae Golf & Country Club
40 Dentonia Park Par 3 Golf Course
41 Don Valley Golf Course

42 Flemingdon Park Golf Club
43 Humber Valley Golf Course
44 Meadowvale Driving Range
45 Morningside Golf Club
46 Parkview Golf Club
47 Tam O'Shanter Golf Club
48 West Hill Golf & Country Club
49 De Havilland Golf Club
50 Scarborough Golf Club
51 Toronto Hunt Golf Club
52 Donalda Club
53 Rosedale Golf Club
54 York Downs Golf Course
55 Northwood Golf Club
56 Oakdale Golf & Country Club
57 Weston Golf & Country Club
58 St. George's Golf & Country Club

59 Lambton Golf Club
60 Islington Golf Club
61 Don Valley Ski Centre
62 Argonaut Rowing Club
63 Balmy Beach Canoe Club
64 Boulevard Club
65 National Yacht Club
66 Queen City Yacht Club
67 Royal Canadian Yacht Club
68 Island Yacht Club
69 Ashbridge's Bay Yacht Club

Centennial Centres
70 North York
71 Scarborough

Broadcasting Centres
72 CTV
73 CBC

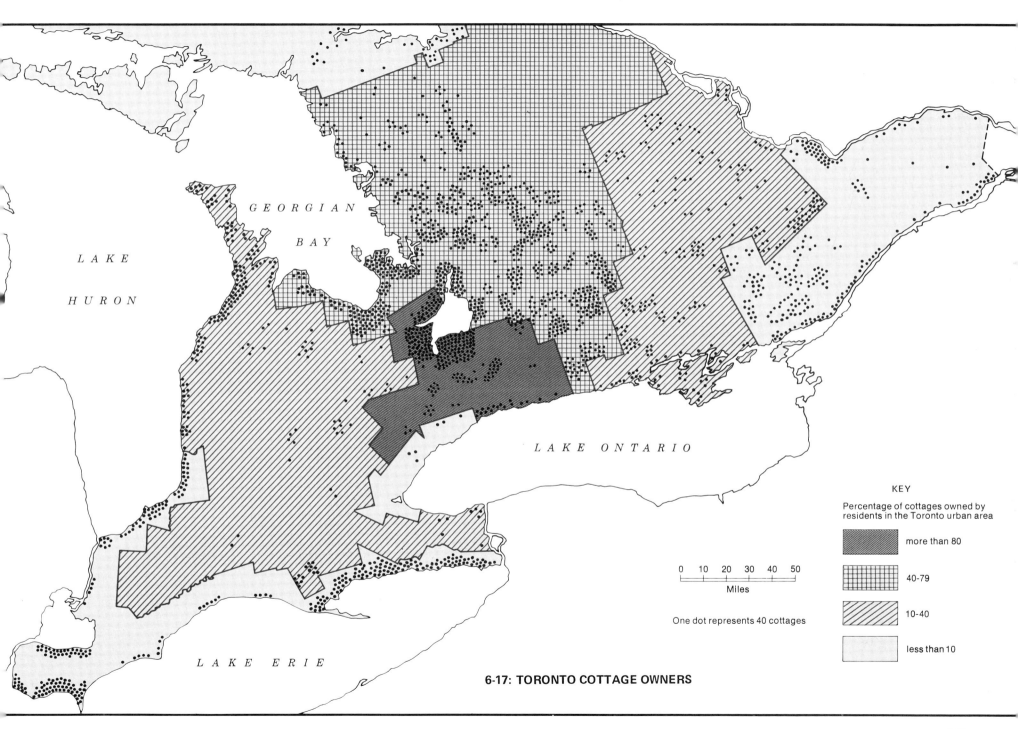

KEY

Percentage of cottages owned by
residents in the Toronto urban area

more than 80

40-79

10-40

less than 10

0 10 20 30 40 50

Miles

One dot represents 40 cottages

6-17: TORONTO COTTAGE OWNERS

LAKE HURON

GEORGIAN BAY

LAKE ONTARIO

LAKE ERIE

THE AIR POLLUTION PROBLEM

Air pollution is of concern to everyone because we all contribute to it and we all suffer from it.

The most important (or the worst) centres for air pollution today are the large cities. It is in these cities that there are the greatest concentrations of the major sources of pollution—automobiles, industries, incinerators and thermal-electric generating stations. From these sources soot, sulphur gas, carbon monoxide and several other pollutants are emitted.

It is difficult to show direct relationships between any particular pollutant and health conditions, but the combination of various pollutants in unusually high concentrations can produce noticeable ill effects. On the basis of reliable statistical studies the following disease groups are significantly correlated to urban living:

> cancer of the oesophagus and stomach
> cancer of the trachea, bronchus and lung
> heart disease

Today the automobile is the greatest single cause of air pollution. It produces more pollutants by weight than all other pollution sources combined. It affects not only those areas which are near traffic streams, it also contributes greatly to pollution levels over the urban area as a whole.

Weather conditions have very strong effects on the quality of our air. Pollutants can be carried for great distances at high altitudes by winds, and on windy days pollutants tend to be blown away and diluted. At certain times, however, when a layer of warm air lies over the city, the lower air cannot rise very high and pollutants in the air form a thick pall or haze. This condition is called an *inversion*. When fog forms at the same time *smog* (smoke plus fog) is created. Fortunately, inversions in Toronto usually do not last very long because the city's weather changes fairly regularly and quickly.

Aware of the increasing seriousness of the air pollution problem, the Ontario Government in 1967 passed the Air Pollution Control Act. Many people feel today, however, that not nearly enough is being done about this problem. In 1969, a group based in the University of Toronto, called "Pollution Probe," was formed. "Pollution Probe" is dedicated to stepped-up action in solving the pollution problem.

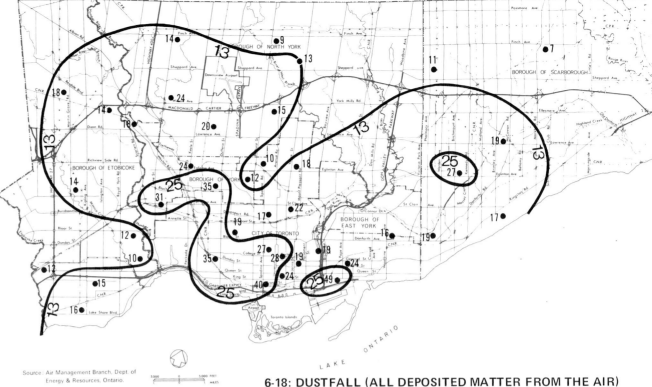

Source: Air Management Branch, Dept. of Energy & Resources, Ontario.

6-18: DUSTFALL (ALL DEPOSITED MATTER FROM THE AIR) FOR THE YEAR 1969 IN TONS PER SQUARE MILE PER MONTH

The Globe and Mail, Toronto

6-19: Pollution haze over Toronto, April 28, 1970

Ontario's Air Pollution Index and Alert System

An Air Pollution Index was established by the Ontario Government in March 1970 to provide the public with a day to day knowledge of pollution levels and to give warning of, and to prevent the adverse effects of, a build-up of air pollution which may occur during prolonged periods of stagnant weather. Legislation in the Province of Ontario authorizes the Minister of Energy and Resources Management to order the curtailment or shutdown of any source of pollution not essential to public health or safety should pollution reach the level which would be injurious to the health of the citizens in the community.

In order that it be used as one of the bases of such control, the Air Pollution Index was designed to be readily comparable with the levels which were reached during "Air Pollution Episodes." During these episodes, which occurred in the past in other parts of the world, air pollution caused an increase in human sickness and mortality for people with respiratory problems. Another basis of pollution control, used in conjunction with the Index, is the meteorological forecast. When the meteorological forecast indicates that high pollution potential conditions will persist for at least six hours the Government can order sources of pollution to curtail their operations.

The Ontario Air Pollution Index is based on the continuous measurements of sulphur dioxide and suspended particulate matter. Measurements of these pollutants are taken at various field stations throughout the province and are telemetered to the Air Management Head Office of the Ontario Department of Energy and Resources.

For a downtown Toronto location the equation for the Air Pollution Index is as follows:

$$API = .2(30.5\ COH + 126.0\ SO_2)^{1.35}$$

where COH = 24-hour running average of the soiling Index
  expressed as Coefficient of Haze per a thousand linear feet
  SO_2 = 24-hour running average of sulphur dioxide concentrations in parts per million.

An Air Pollution Index of less than 32 is considered acceptable. At these levels concentrations of sulphur dioxide and particulates should have little or no effect on human health. At the Advisory Level, at which the Air Pollution Index is equal to 32 and meteorological conditions are expected to remain adverse for at least six more hours, owners of significant sources of pollution in the community may be advised to make preparation for the curtailment of their operations.

The First Alert occurs when the Air Pollution Index reaches 50 and adverse weather is forecast to continue for at least six hours. The Minister may order major sources to curtail their activities. Studies have shown that at levels over 50, patients with chronic respiratory diseases may experience an accentuation in symptoms.

If the abatement action does not succeed in lowering the pollution levels and the Index rises to 75, the Second Alert is issued. The Minister may order sources to make further curtailment in operations. When the Index reaches 100, the Air Pollution Episode Threshold Level, the Minister may require the curtailment of all sources not essential to public health or safety. At this level the air pollution could have mild effects on healthy people and might seriously endanger those with severe cardiac or respiratory disease.

Source: L. Shenfeld, Ontario Department of Energy and Resources Management, Air Management Branch

Another Pollution Problem

6-21: "... there's a note in this bottle from a Mrs. Haroldson, upstream somewhere ... says she's sorry about the detergent she's emptying into the river, but her husband likes a complete change of clothes daily and ... "

Reprinted with permission of *Toronto Daily Star*

1968 Motor Vehicle Registrations—Metropolitan Toronto and the Province of Ontario

	Passenger	Dual Purpose	Truck & Tractor*	Total
Metropolitan Toronto	648,063	57,418	79,459	784,940
Ontario	2,237,298	187,618	385,242	2,810,158

*Estimated   Source: Department of Transport, Ontario

6-20: THE MOTOR VEHICLE'S CONTRIBUTION TO FIVE MAJOR AIR CONTAMINANTS

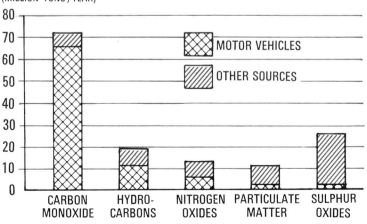

ANNUAL EMISSIONS (MILLION TONS /YEAR)

⊠ MOTOR VEHICLES
▨ OTHER SOURCES

CARBON MONOXIDE | HYDRO-CARBONS | NITROGEN OXIDES | PARTICULATE MATTER | SULPHUR OXIDES

SECTION 7 SPHERES OF INFLUENCE

A city is normally the centre or nucleus of a large area which it dominates. With distance outward from the centre, the influence of the city weakens and eventually is exceeded by the influence of some other city.

The boundary of an area of dominance is exceedingly difficult to define. What the area consists of, in reality, is a number of single-feature areas: the city newspaper circulation area, the retail and wholesale trade area, the commuting area, and so on. Some of these single-feature regions extend well beyond the boundary of the city's area of over-all dominance, while others fall short of it. A metropolis such as Toronto, then, not only exerts influence over its area of dominance, but can strongly influence certain economic activities on a national and international scale as well.

The materials that follow provide direct evidence of Toronto's influence as a major centre. Materials on several other pages in this book also reflect that influence, although somewhat less directly, and should therefore be considered along with the materials in this section.

Focal points

— The evidence of Toronto's role as a centre of influence in the South-central Ontario region, Southern Ontario as a whole, and at the national and international scale
— Features in the landscape of Toronto that have resulted from its role as a major centre of influence
— The effects that the continued rapid growth of Toronto could have on the South-central Ontario region, Southern Ontario as a whole, and other parts of Canada

7-1: One Method of Determining the Position of the Retail Breaking Point Between Two Cities*

The *retail breaking point* between any two cities is the point out to which one city dominates retail trade and beyond which the other city dominates.

Let us say that there are two cities, A and B. The number of miles between them is 250. A has a population of 500,000, B a population of 150,000. The number of miles from A to the outer limit of the area in which it dominates retail trade, computed along a major paved highway running from A to B, is

$$\frac{\text{number of miles between A and B (250)}}{1 + \sqrt{\dfrac{\text{population of B (150,000)}}{\text{population of A (500,000)}}}} = 161.6$$

That is, the retail breaking point between A and B is, expectedly, much nearer the smaller city.

---

* This method of determining the retail breaking point between two cities is a simplification of William J. Reilly's *Law of Retail Gravitation,* presented by Frank Strohkarck and Katherine Phelps in an article entitled "The Mechanics of Constructing a Market Area Map," *Journal of Marketing,* Vol. 12, pp. 493-496, 1948.

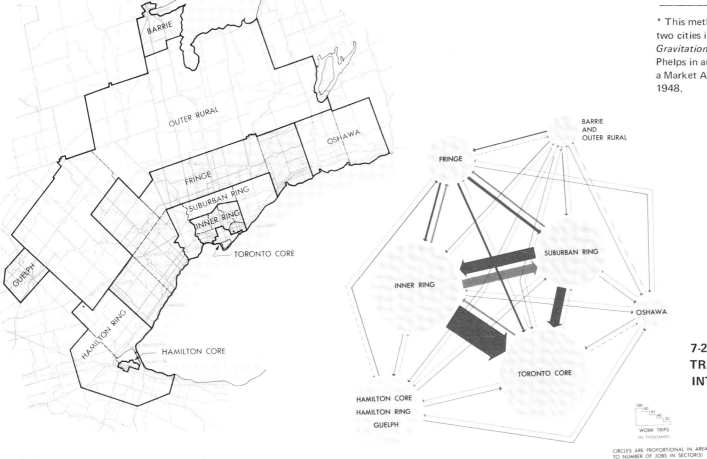

7-2: METROPOLITAN TORONTO AND REGION TRANSPORTATION STUDY (MTARTS): INTERCHANGE OF WORKERS

WORK TRIPS
(IN THOUSANDS)

CIRCLES ARE PROPORTIONAL IN AREA
TO NUMBER OF JOBS IN SECTOR(S)

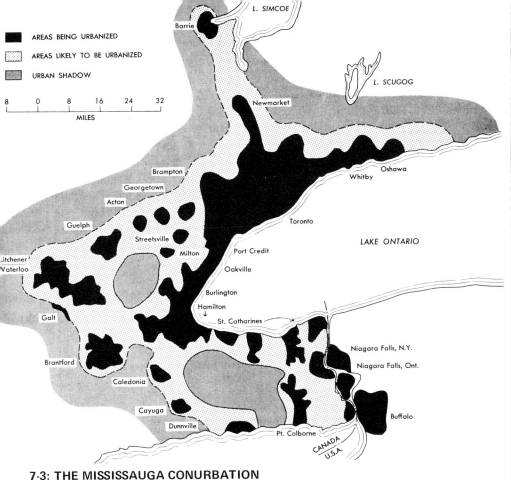

8 0 8 16 24 32

MILES

7-3: THE MISSISSAUGA CONURBATION

Every village, town, or city becomes to some degree, a central place that dominates the trading or commercial activities of a fairly large area around it. It usually develops as the principal market for goods produced in the surrounding area and as the area's principal distribution centre as well, providing storage, transportation, and administrative services. Such a surrounding area is called by some geographers the centre's *umland,* by other geographers its *hinterland.* Because business from an umland or hinterland "flows" or feeds into a central place, these areas are often called *tributary areas,* as well.

Shown on Map 7-4 are places in Southern Ontario which had a population of 1,000 or more in 1961 and which contained various wholesale establishments (establishments that sell goods to retail establishments, not directly to consumers). As the map key indicates, these places have been classed on the basis of the number of wholesale establishments they contain. No attempt has been made to indicate the size of the various establishments, but as a general rule the larger establishments are located in larger places. Each place is the centre of wholesale trading activities for a considerable tributary area. Furthermore, each centre functions at all the class levels up to which it is classed. Ottawa, for example, a Class II centre, performs the wholesale functions of a Class V, Class IV, and a Class III centre as well as for a Class II centre. Its tributary area includes several lower class centres and their relatively small tributary areas.

Only the boundaries of the tributary areas of Class II centres are shown. This gives a picture of the spheres of influence of the major wholesale centres in Southern Ontario.

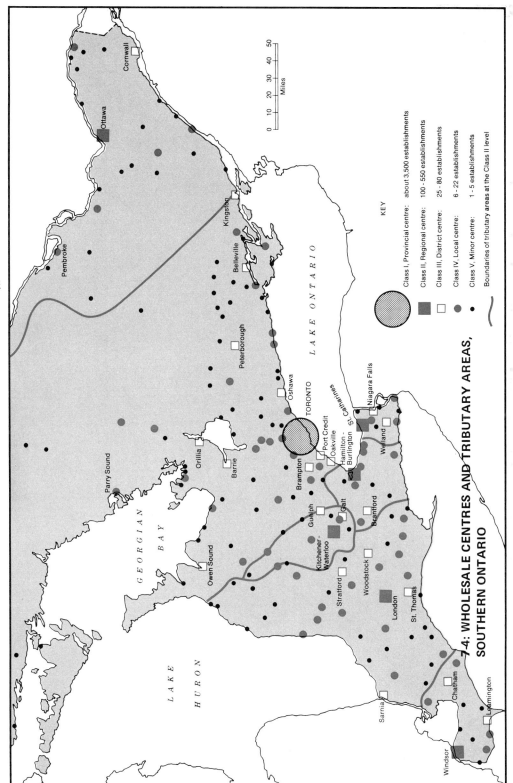

7-4: WHOLESALE CENTRES AND TRIBUTARY AREAS, SOUTHERN ONTARIO

KEY

Class I, Provincial centre: about 3,500 establishments

Class II, Regional centre: 100 - 550 establishments

Class III, District centre: 25 - 80 establishments

Class IV, Local centre: 6 - 22 establishments

Class V, Minor centre: 1 - 5 establishments

Boundaries of tributary areas at the Class II level

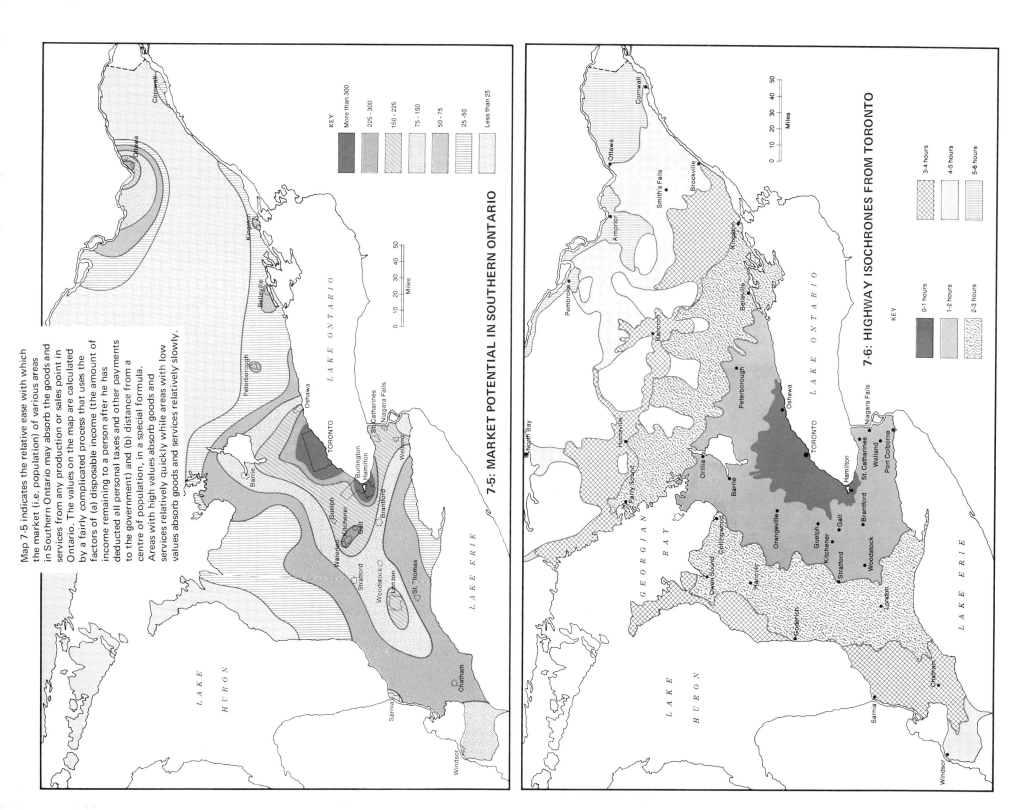

Map 7-5 indicates the relative ease with which the market (i.e. population) of various areas in Southern Ontario may absorb the goods and services from any production or sales point in Ontario. The values on the map are calculated by a fairly complicated process that uses the factors of (a) disposable income (the amount of income remaining to a person after he has deducted all personal taxes and other payments to the government) and (b) distance from a centre of population, in a special formula. Areas with high values absorb goods and services relatively quickly while areas with low values absorb goods and services relatively slowly.

7-5: MARKET POTENTIAL IN SOUTHERN ONTARIO

KEY

	More than 300
	225 - 300
	150 - 225
	75 - 150
	50 - 75
	25 - 50
	Less than 25

Miles
0 10 20 30 40 50

LAKE HURON

LAKE ERIE

LAKE ONTARIO

Windsor
Sarnia
Chatham
St. Thomas
London
Woodstock
Stratford
Waterloo
Galt
Kitchener
Guelph
Brantford
Barrie
Hamilton
Burlington
TORONTO
Welland
Niagara Falls
St. Catharines
Oshawa
Peterborough
Belleville
Kingston
Ottawa
Cornwall

7-6: HIGHWAY ISOCHRONES FROM TORONTO

KEY

	0-1 hours
	1-2 hours
	2-3 hours
	3-4 hours
	4-5 hours
	5-6 hours

Miles
0 10 20 30 40 50

LAKE HURON

LAKE ERIE

GEORGIAN BAY

LAKE ONTARIO

Windsor
Sarnia
Chatham
London
Godrich
Woodstock
Stratford
Owen Sound
Hanover
Collingwood
Orangeville
Kitchener
Guelph
Galt
Brantford
St. Catharines
Welland
Port Colborne
Niagara Falls
Hamilton
TORONTO
Orillia
Barrie
Oshawa
Peterborough
Parry Sound
Huntsville
North Bay
Bancroft
Belleville
Kingston
Pembroke
Arnprior
Smith's Falls
Brockville
Ottawa
Cornwall

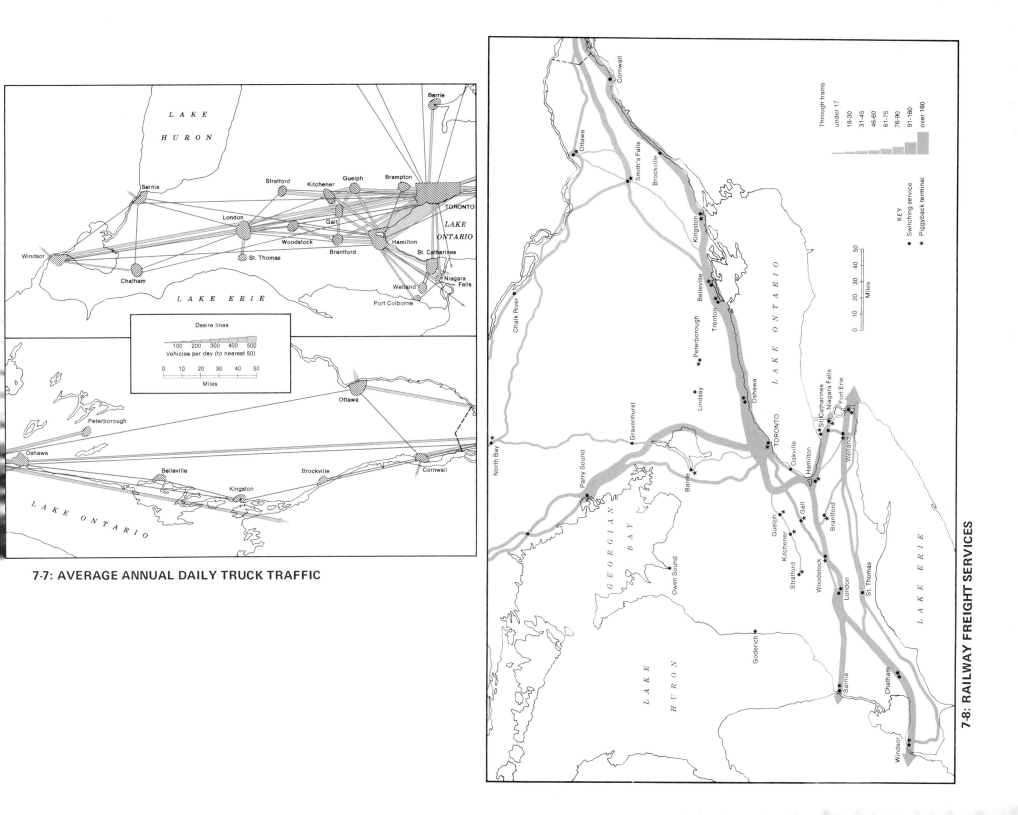

7-7: AVERAGE ANNUAL DAILY TRUCK TRAFFIC

7-8: RAILWAY FREIGHT SERVICES

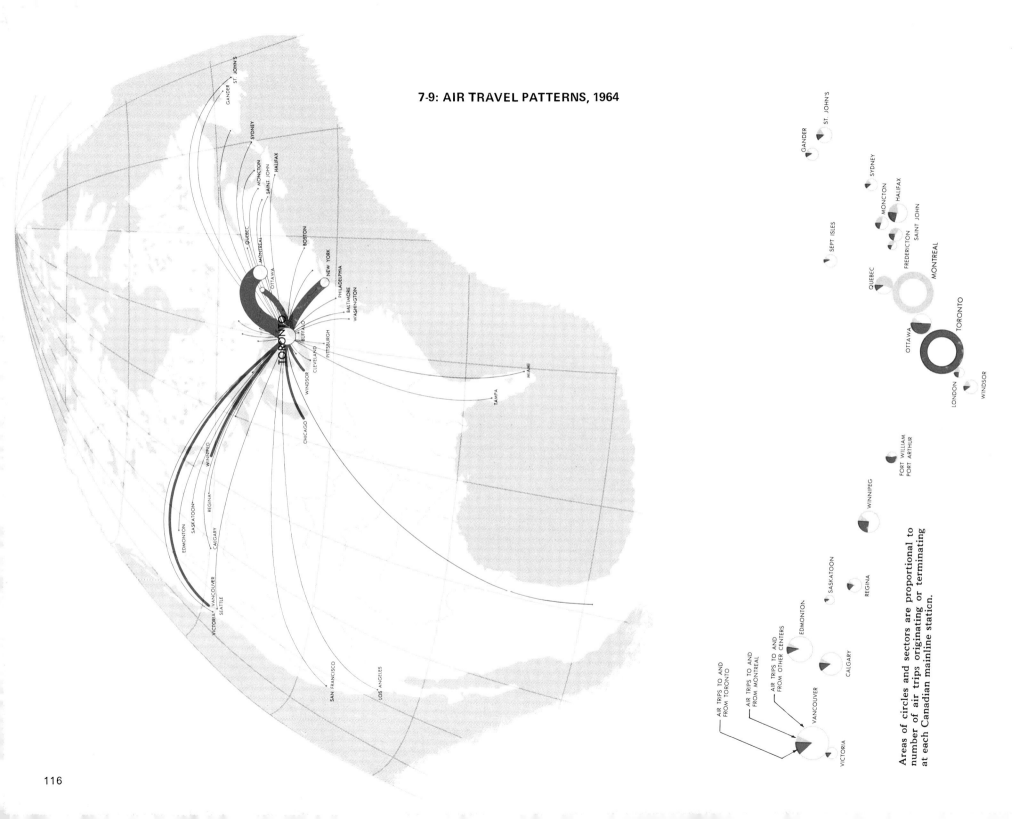

7-9: AIR TRAVEL PATTERNS, 1964

Areas of circles and sectors are proportional to number of air trips originating or terminating at each Canadian mainline station.

AIR TRIPS TO AND FROM TORONTO

AIR TRIPS TO AND FROM MONTREAL

AIR TRIPS TO AND FROM OTHER CENTERS

7-10: *Toronto International Airport*
7-11: *Aerial view of Toronto Harbour, showing the new outer harbour headland extension, Toronto Islands (upper left) and Toronto Island Airport*
7-12: *The Docks*
7-13: *The Ontario Food Terminal*
7-14: *Railway Marshalling Yards, northern fringe*

7-13

7-14

7-15: CARGOES LOADED AND UNLOADED AT 5 PRINCIPAL CANADIAN PORTS 1966

Rank by total tonnage		International		Coastwise		Total
		Loaded tons	Unloaded tons	Loaded tons	Unloaded tons	tons
		'000	'000	'000	'000	'000
1	Montreal	5,548	6,475	4,603	6,210	22,836
2	Vancouver	10,409	1,859	5,427	3,957	21,652
5	Hamilton	191	7,320	504	2,703	10,719
7	Halifax	2,846	4,228	1,950	383	9,407
10	Toronto	223	3,159	277	1,935	5,595
Total — All Canadian Ports		83,987	53,020	60,762	60,686	258,455

Source: Canada Year Book, 1968

7-16: SOME BASIC FACTS ABOUT THE PORT OF TORONTO 1968 SHIPPING SEASON

Length of 1968 shipping season:
273 days (beginning April 2)
No. of countries from which
imports arrived: 59
No. of countries to which
exports were shipped: 65
Leading countries from which
foreign ships arrived:
West Germany: 72 ships, 215 calls
United Kingdom: 55 ships,
184 calls
Norway: 59 ships, 156 calls
No. of vessels remaining in port for
winter lay-up: 45
No. of over-the-road vehicles handled:
104,847
No. of railway cars handled: 434
No. of aircraft movements at
Toronto Island Airport: 214,710

Source: The Port of Toronto

7-17: THE PORT OF TORONTO

	TRAFFIC			DIRECT OVERSEAS SHIPPING		
Year	Cargo Tonnage	Vessel Arrivals and Departures	Year	No. of Regular Liner Services Serving the Port	Total No. of Arrivals and Departures of Ships	Total Cargo Tonnage
1912	343,608	No record	1956	20	910	164,929
*1929	959,234	4,270	1957	24	1,046	200,395
**1931	2,122,066	5,038	1958	28	1,317	287,768
1963	6,421,893	4,532	*1959	40	1,724	713,186
1964	5,673,632	4,065	1963	48	1,988	1,045,262
1965	6,070,743	3,962	1964	53	2,157	1,232,349
1966	5,701,202	3,914	1965	55	2,276	1,489,022
1967	5,694,024	3,816	1966	56	2,288	1,462,245
1968	6,071,061	3,258	1967	56	2,374	1,497,187
Cargo figures are in short tons			1968	41	1,788	1,393,763

*Year previous to opening of New Welland Canal   *First Year New St. Lawrence Seaway

**First full year of operation of New Welland Canal

Source: The Port of Toronto

7-18: THE LOCATION OF UNITED STATES SUBSIDIARIES IN SOUTHERN ONTARIO BY SUB-REGIONS

United States Standard Metropolitan Statistical Area	Number of establishments 1958	Distance from Toronto by air (km)	Eastern Ontario	Lake Ontario	Metropolitan Toronto	Burlington	Niagara	Lake Erie	Lake St. Clair Border	Lake St. Clair Lambton	Upper Grand River	Georgian Bay	Northern Ontario	Total Ontario
Akron	698	336			9	2	1	1			1			14
Boston	5,665	690		2	8	4								14
Buffalo	1,820	96		1	10	2	17	1			3			34
Chicago	13,508	702	5	7	98	11	3	6	5	6	4	2		147
Cincinnati	1,776	660		1	12	2		2	1					18
Cleveland	3,898	306			28	9	6	1	1	1	3	1		50
Columbus	835	506			7	6	1							15
Detroit	6,468	340	1	4	26	6	1	3	37	1	9	1		89
Los Angeles	16,910	3,496			28	1	1	1					2	35
Milwaukee	2,298	693			10	1	1					1		13
Minn.-St. Paul	2,433	1,111			13	1	1	1			1			19
Newark	4,425	539			14	2		2				2		20
New York	39,396	557	7	7	145	12	8	11	3		11	3	3	210
Philadelphia	8,124	534		2	19	5	1	5			2		1	33
Pittsburgh	2,479	363			19	4	2	4		1	7	1		38
Rochester	1,015	152		1	10	2								13
St. Louis	3,150	1,065		2	13	1	1	4	2	2	5			29
Toledo	742	409		1	7	1	1	1	2	1	1			15
Total			24	28	469	62	42	40	54	15	48	18	6	806

Source: Gentilcore, R. Louis (Editor), *Canada's Changing Geography*, Prentice-Hall of Canada, Ltd., Page 154.

7-19: CIRCULATION OF TORONTO'S DAILY NEWSPAPERS

(Monday to Saturday Circulation averages as of Sept. 30, 1969)

	The Globe and Mail (morning)	% of Total Average Paid Circulation	Toronto Daily Star (evening)	% of Total Average Paid Circulation	The Telegram (evening)	% of Total Average Paid Circulation
Total Average Paid Circulation	261,803	100	386,013	100	242,652	100
City Zone Circulation	119,581	45	265,764	69	154,683	64
Retail Trading Zone Circulation	39,214	15	73,454	19	52,091	21
Circulation Areas Outside City Zone and Retail Trading Zone	103,008	40	46,795	12	35,878	15

Source: Publisher's Statements: The **Globe and Mail, Toronto Daily Star** and The **Telegram**

7-20: CIRCULATION OF DAILY NEWSPAPERS TORONTO, MONTREAL, AND VANCOUVER, SPRING 1970

Total Average Paid Circulation
(Monday to Saturday)

TORONTO
The *Globe and Mail*	269,698
Toronto Daily Star	386,013
The *Telegram*	242,652

MONTREAL
Le Devoir		36,280
The *Gazette*		132,738
Le Journal de Montréal		52,052
Montréal-Matin	Monday to Friday	144,191
La Presse		205,158
The *Star*		187,302

VANCOUVER
The *Sun*	254,033
The *Province*	115,536

Source: Canadian Advertising Rates and Data, May 1970

— Metropolitan Toronto has 7 Canadian charter banks which include 650 branch offices, 49 trust companies, and 68 life insurance companies.
— Metropolitan Toronto houses 34% of Canada's advertising agencies, 28% of its management consultants, 30% of its consulting engineering firms, 22% of its manufacturers' agents, 54% of its mining companies' head offices, 41% of its motion picture companies and studios, and 24% of its stock and bond brokerage houses.

Source: Ontario Department of Trade and Development, Trade and Industry Division.

7-21: VALUE OF TRADING — 1969

The Toronto Stock Exchange and Leading U.S. Stock Exchanges

	$
1. New York Stock Exchange	129,603,000,000
2. American Stock Exchange (New York)	30,074,000,000
3. Midwest Stock Exchange (Chicago)	5,988,000,000
4. Toronto Stock Exchange	5,765,000,000
5. Pacific Coast Stock Exchange (Los Angeles)	5,422,000,000
6. Philadelphia-Baltimore-Washington Stock Exchange	2,528,000,000

The Toronto Stock Exchange and Other Leading Canadian Stock Exchanges

	$
1. Toronto Stock Exchange	5,765,000,000
2. Montreal Stock Exchange and the Canadian Stock Exchange, combined (both in Montreal)	1,628,000,000
3. Vancouver Stock Exchange	1,148,000,000
4. Calgary Stock Exchange	76,600,000
5. Winnipeg Stock Exchange	5,800,000
Total — All Canadian Stock Exchanges	8,624,000,000

Note: The Toronto Stock Exchange has a high proportion of listings which are valuable industrial stocks. The Toronto value, therefore, is correspondingly higher than for centres with lower proportions of industrial listings.

Source: The Toronto Stock Exchange

7-22: LABOUR FORCE, 15 YEARS OF AGE AND OVER, BY SELECTED OCCUPATIONS, TORONTO CENSUS METROPOLITAN AREA, MONTREAL CENSUS METROPOLITAN AREA, ONTARIO, AND CANADA, 1961

Occupation	Toronto CMA		Montreal CMA		Ontario		Canada	
	Male	Female	Male	Female	Male	Female	Male	Female
Managerial Occupations	73,031	6,658	67,061	6,335	188,666	20,866	481,379	57,661
Professional Engineers	8,540	33	8,819	48	19,676	53	42,950	116
Law Professionals	2,587	99	1,986	44	5,010	174	12,594	328
Physicians & Surgeons	2,815	342	3,436	292	7,408	632	19,835	1,455
Artists, Writers & Musicians	5,165	2,045	4,481	1,707	8,922	4,901	19,934	11,818
Architects	664	12	669	26	1,117	21	2,874	66
Printers, Bookbinders and Related Workers	9,064	1,738	6,464	1,230	15,490	3,178	31,556	6,442
Professors & College Principals	944	249	1,616	649	2,562	490	8,779	2,366

Source: 1961 Census of Canada

SECTION 8 PLANNING THE CITY OF THE FUTURE

Planning is a slow and extremely complex process. The materials in this section provide nothing more than a glimpse of the work that an organization such as the Metropolitan Planning Board has done and continues to do in its efforts to design a better city. The following pages, however, do reveal something very basic about the planning process: planning is carried on simultaneously at several levels and what is done at one level must be co-ordinated with what is done at the other levels if any measure of success is to be gained.

Focal points

— Evidence of the need for planning in the Toronto area
— Toronto's existing (1968) general land use pattern compared to the *Development Plan: General Concept* prepared by the Metropolitan Toronto Planning Board
— The effects on Toronto and its region of the new *Toronto-centred Region Concept*
— Evidence of the effects of former planning measures in Toronto
— The ways in which a planning organization might use various materials in this book
— Steps involved in planning particular areas within the city and the city as a whole
— The problems of having different levels of planning
— Plans that you would create for parts of Toronto and for the city as a whole

8-1: A suggested plan for the development of part of downtown and the waterfront: Project Toronto (model superimposed on a photograph of the city), designed by Fuller-Sadao (Buckminster Fuller)/Geometrics, Architects, Engineers, Planners, Cambridge, Mass., May 1968; sponsored by The Toronto Telegram and CFTO-TV, Toronto. A long "galleria" containing a minirail, shops, galleries, restaurants and cinemas runs along the east side of an extended University Avenue and is linked at several points to buildings nearby. The most prominent building is the white Gateway Office Tower.

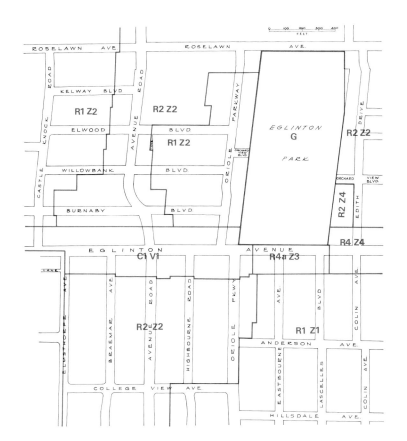

AN EXAMPLE OF ZONING: CITY OF TORONTO

PERMISSIBLE USES

	G.	R.1	R.1A	R.1F	R.2	R.3	R.4	R.4A		C.1A	C.1S	C.1	A.C.	
Residential Districts										**Commercial Districts**				
Park-Playground	●	●	●	●	●	●	●	●				●	○	All Residential Buildings
Community Centre	●	○	○	○	○	●	●	●		●	●		○	Some Residential Buildings
Church		○	○	●	●	●	●	●		○	○	●	●	Public Buildings
Detached Dwelling		●	●	●	●	●	●	●		●		●	○	Institutions
Doctor, Dentist		○	○	○	○	○	●	●		●	●	●	○	Office Building
Semi-detached Dwelling			●	●	●	●	●	●		●		●	○	Hospital
Duplex			○	●	●	●	●	●		●	●	●	○	Bank
Double Duplex			○	●	●	●	●	●			●	●	○	Hotel
Triplex				●	●	●	●	●		○	●	●	○	Restaurant
Double Triplex				●	●	●	●	●			●	●	○	Theatre, Hall
Row House				●	●	●	●	●			●	●	○	Commercial Club
Apartment House			○		○	○	●	●				●	○	Place of Amusement
Converted Dwelling			○		○	●	●	●			●	●	○	Retail Store
Boarding House				○	○	●	●	●			○	●	○	Personal Service Shop
Parking Station				○	○	○	○	○			●	●	○	Bake-Shop
Nursing Home				○	●	●	●	●			○	●	○	Repair and Service Shop
Day Nursery				○	○	●	●	●			○	●	○	Studio, Custom Workshop
Children's Home					○	●	●	●		●		●	○	Commercial School
Boys' Home					○	●	●	●		●		●	○	Supermarket
Public School		○	○	○	○	●	●	●			○	○		Animal Hospital
Private School				○	○	●	●	●		●	●		○	Private Parking Garage
Public Hospital						●	●	●				●	○	Public Parking Garage
Private Club						●	●	●			●	●	●	Service Station
Fraternity House						●	●	●			●	●	○	Used Car Lot
Public Library						●	●	●						
YMCA, etc.						●	●	●						
Institutional Office							●	●						
Professional Office							●	●						
Administrative Office							●	●						
Office Bldg. for above Offices							●	●						

● Permitted ○ Permitted subject to restrictions in By-Law

PERMISSIBLE DENSITIES

Zone 1	Zone 2	Zone 3	Zone 4	Zone 5
0.35	0.6	1.0	2.0	2.5

L1	L2	L3	L4 (through)	L9
1.0	2.0	3.0	4.0	9.0

V1	V2	V3	V4
3.0	5.0	7.0	12.0

The table indicates generally the kinds of uses permitted in each zoning category. The uses listed are representative: most of the residential, but only some of the commercial and industrial uses are shown. The Zoning By-Law recognizes several hundred specific uses and for accurate information reference should be made to it.

Where the table shows that restrictions apply, there may be any of several kinds: on location, standards, design, or the nature of the use. Once again, the By-Law is the source of accurate information.

The Zoning By-Law assigns to each lot a floor area ratio which, when multiplied by the area of the lot, gives the maximum permissible floor space.

To find the permissible amount of floor space on any lot, check the map in By-Law 20623 and note which of the designations in the diagram has been applied to the lot. If the lot is to be used for a residential building it will be a "Zone" designation; if for an office or commercial building it will be either an "L" or "V" designation. Find the ratio that corresponds to the designation and multiply it by the area of the lot.

To give an idea of the range of densities permitted by the ratios, the striped rectangles each represent a lot and the solid ones the amount of floor space that the ratios permit on such a lot.

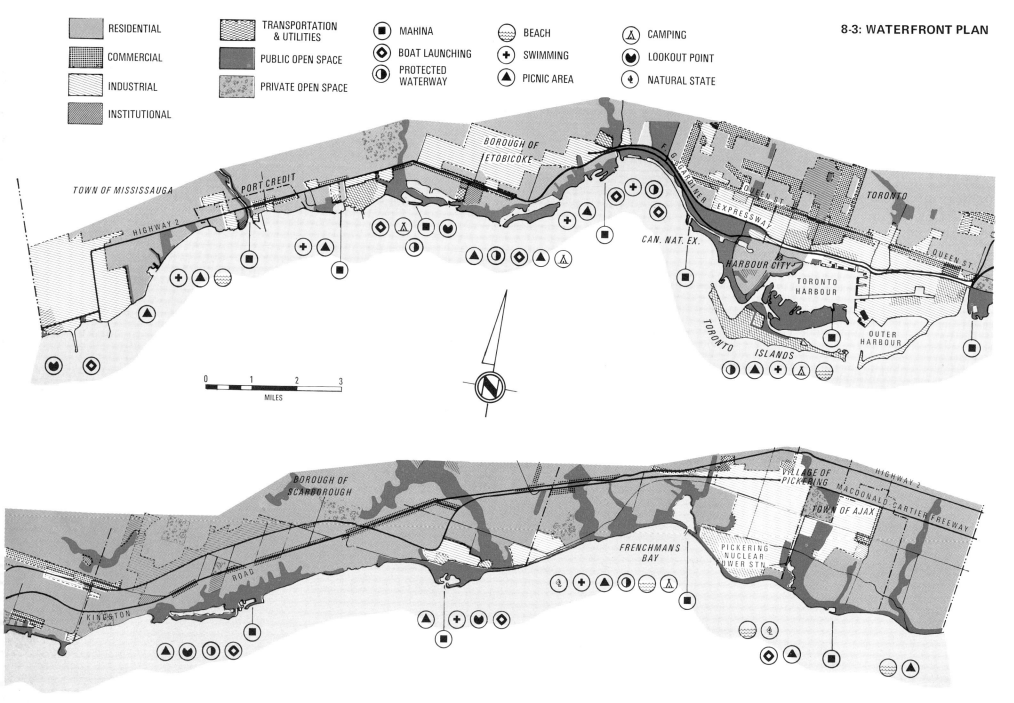

RESIDENTIAL

COMMERCIAL

INDUSTRIAL

INSTITUTIONAL

TRANSPORTATION
& UTILITIES

PUBLIC OPEN SPACE

PRIVATE OPEN SPACE

MARINA

BOAT LAUNCHING

PROTECTED
WATERWAY

BEACH

SWIMMING

PICNIC AREA

CAMPING

LOOKOUT POINT

NATURAL STATE

8-3: WATERFRONT PLAN

TOWN OF MISSISSAUGA

PORT CREDIT

HIGHWAY 2

BOROUGH OF
ETOBICOKE

F. G. GARDINER

EXPRESSWAY

QUEEN ST.

TORONTO

QUEEN ST.

CAN. NAT. EX.

HARBOUR CITY

TORONTO
HARBOUR

OUTER
HARBOUR

TORONTO

TORONTO
ISLANDS

0   1   2   3
MILES

N

BOROUGH OF
SCARBOROUGH

VILLAGE OF
PICKERING

HIGHWAY 2

MACDONALD CARTIER FREEWAY

TOWN OF AJAX

FRENCHMANS
BAY

PICKERING
NUCLEAR
POWER STN.

ROAD

KINGSTON

122

Few large cities are blessed with a lakefront location. Not until recently, however, has Toronto made the necessary long-range, comprehensive plans to redevelop its waterfront so that it might become an area that could be used by all in a variety of ways. Recognizing the tremendous importance of the waterfront to the development of the city, the Metropolitan Toronto Planning Board initiated a study of the part of the Lake Ontario shoreline that lies within the Metropolitan Toronto Planning Area. This study eventually led to the design of a waterfront plan. The principal objectives of the plan as originally conceived are

   modernization and expansion of Toronto harbour

   redevelopment or replacement of obsolete industrial and commercial installations

   provision of land for industries and utilities requiring lakeside location

   provision of land for a more efficient and accessible downtown airport

   provision of land for expansion and revitalization of the Canadian National Exhibition

   development and redevelopment of residential areas to take advantage of their lakefront setting

   provision of additional land for water-oriented recreational purposes

   expansion of public swimming and bathing facilities, including beaches, pools and artificial lakes

   extension of protected waterways for small boats

   development of additional marinas and boat-launching sites at strategic locations across the waterfront

   provision of aquatic regatta facilities to Olympic specifications

   improvement of public access to the Toronto Islands, while maintaining them for use, primarily, by pedestrians

   construction of a scenic drive linking major points of interest and activity

Map 8-3 shows the principal features of the plan.

8-4. The south side of Queen Street in 1959. The vacant area and parking lots immediately this side of Queen Street are now occupied by the new City Hall and Civic Square.

8-5: Plan for the south side of Queen Street opposite the new City Hall and Civic Square

8-6: POPULATION AND DENSITY			
Planning District	1965 Population	Future Population	Future Density Persons/Acre
1	125,800	142,000	97
2	240,800	260,300	62
3	232,600	274,000	41
4	205,800	245,400	33
5	76,000	133,900	23
6	231,300	259,900	46
7	63,500	68,400	34
8	147,400	193,800	20
9	39,700	74,500	23
10	79,500	155,200	32
11	111,800	170,300	23
12	13,600	88,000	30
13	173,200	219,200	27
14	52,700	94,600	30
15	19,700	105,000	24
16	21,000	227,500	28
Metropolitan Toronto	1,834,400	2,712,000	32

	Urban	Rural	Urban	Rural	
17	26,400	—	252,000	—	20
18	65,100	2,700	290,500	2,700	23
19	2,800	4,800	5,500	4,800	10
20	38,500	5,600	206,000	5,600	17
21	10,900	4,600	35,000	4,600	13
22	1,100	3,300	1,500	3,300	6
23	30,600	1,700	150,000	1,700	19
Fringe Areas	175,400	22,700	940,500	22,700	19
Metropolitan Planning Area	2,009,800	22,700	3,652,500	22,700	27

Source: Metropolitan Toronto Planning Board

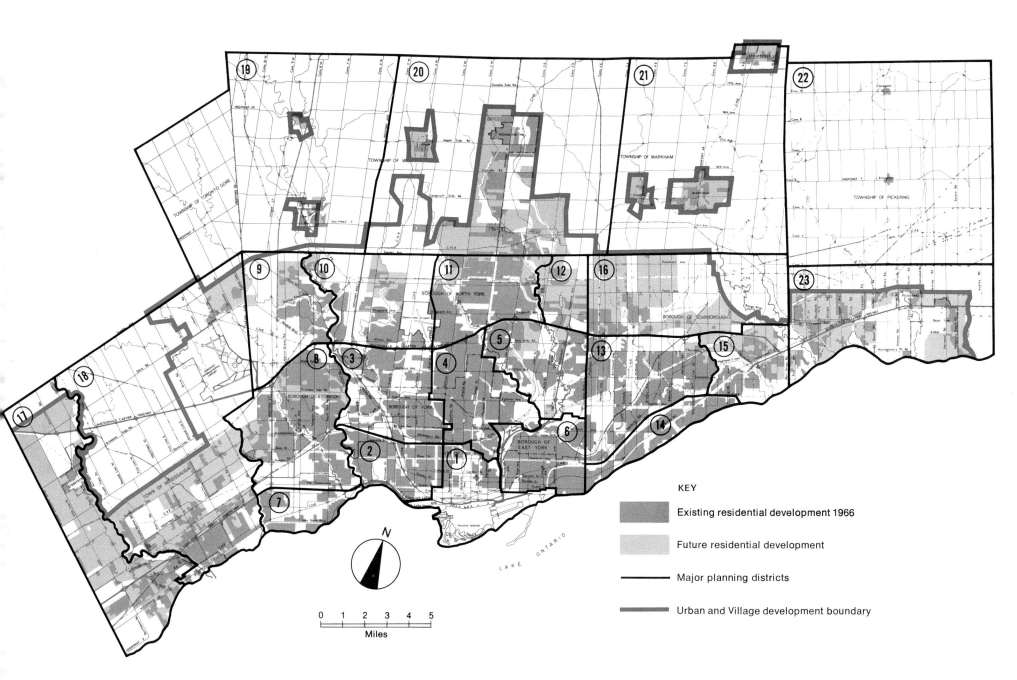

KEY

Existing residential development 1966

Future residential development

Major planning districts

Urban and Village development boundary

0 1 2 3 4 5
Miles

8-7: EXISTING AND FUTURE RESIDENTIAL AREAS, METROPOLITAN TORONTO PLANNING AREA

124

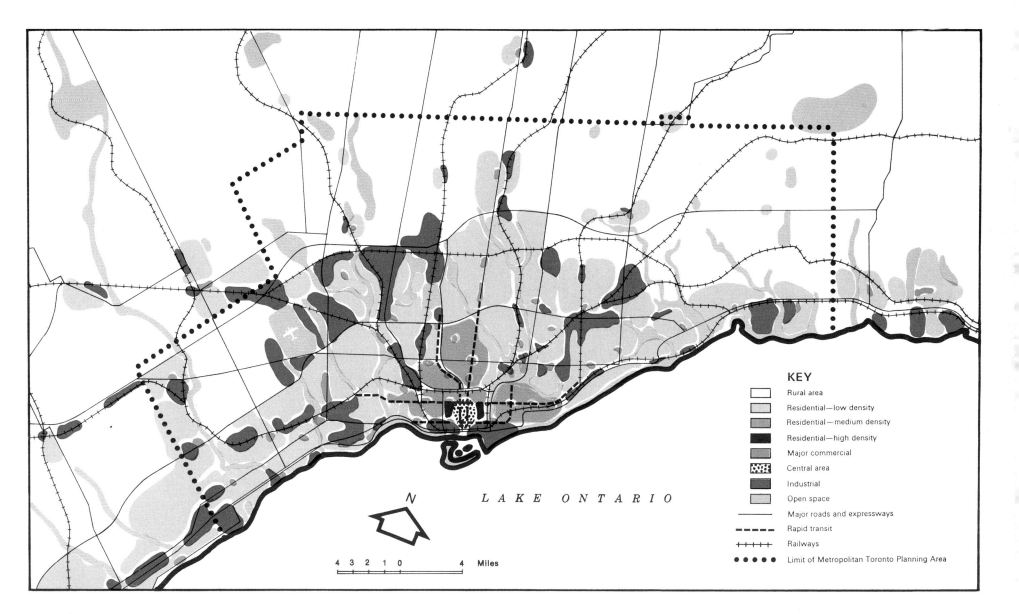

KEY

☐	Rural area
	Residential—low density
	Residential—medium density
■	Residential—high density
	Major commercial
	Central area
	Industrial
	Open space
——	Major roads and expressways
- - - -	Rapid transit
+++++	Railways
●●●●●	Limit of Metropolitan Toronto Planning Area

N

L A K E   O N T A R I O

4 3 2 1 0   4   Miles

8-8: DEVELOPMENT PLAN: GENERAL CONCEPT, METROPOLITAN TORONTO PLANNING BOARD

The Toronto-Centred Region Development Plan

In December 1962, the Government of Ontario
issued an Order-in-Council establishing the
Metropolitan Toronto and Region Transportation Study (MTARTS). From this study
emerged a report entitled *Choices for a
Growing Region*. In the report, broad choices
were proposed for the development of a region
of some 3,200 square miles which included
Metropolitan Toronto and a large surrounding
area. The Government then requested the
submission of public and private briefs so that
it could proceed with an acceptable regional
plan. After careful study of these briefs and
the goals set out in the MTARTS report, the
Government enlarged the MTARTS study area
and named it the Toronto-Centred Region.
In May 1970, a report entitled *Design for
Development: The Toronto-Centred Region*
was issued. The conclusions of this report are
regarded by the Government as basic guidelines
to be followed in all governmental decisions
that may affect the Region.

The Toronto-Centred Region Development
Plan is based on three fundamental objectives:

1. the encouragement of a more even
distribution of people in Ontario
2. the improvement of the quality of life
for those people, and
3. better use of the natural environment.

The present growth trends in the Region,
however, indicate that certain major problems
are developing that would prevent the attainment of those objectives and create a host of
undesirable conditions within the Region itself.

The trends are

rapid population growth within the Region;
the present total population of 3,600,000
(52% of the provincial total and the proportion
is increasing) is expected to rise to 8,000,000
by the year 2000.

growth in the Region is becoming more and
more concentrated in Metropolitan Toronto
and there is a noticeable thrust westward from
the metropolitan core that consists largely
of suburban sprawl

increases in income and in leisure time and
improvements in transportation are making the
Region more accessible and more extensively
used

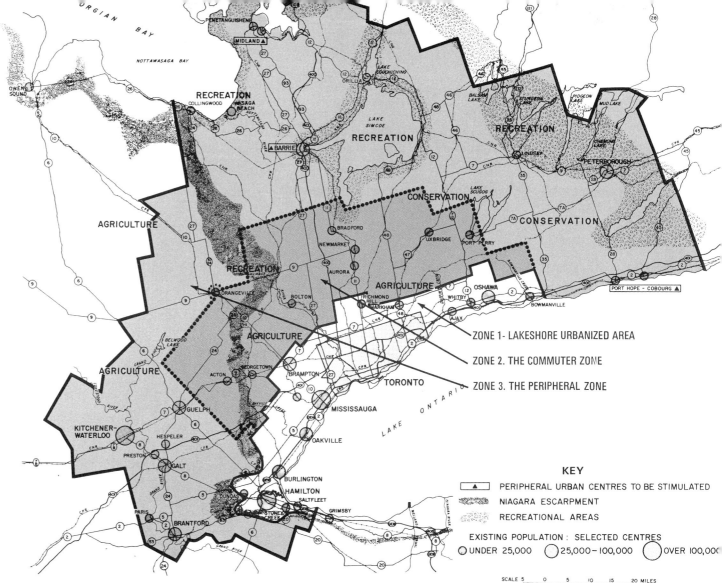

8-9: THE TORONTO-CENTRED REGION DEVELOPMENT PLAN

to the north and east of the metropolitan
core only modest growth is taking place

toward the edges of the Region, summer
residences are taking up large quantities of
land, especially along lakefronts

The major problems that these trends are
creating are

congestion in the urban areas, especially in
the metropolitan core where major difficulties

are developing in housing, traffic, recreation,
air and water pollution, and access to and
from the hinterland

difficulties in providing transportation,
water and sewage services

inefficiency in the use of the Region's
resources

a detraction from the establishment of
strong links between the Region and the
northern and eastern parts of Ontario

To provide a basis for the attainment of
their fundamental objectives and the development of solutions to these problems, the
Government of Ontario has designed a three-
tiered Region: Zone 1—The Lakeshore
Urbanized Area; Zone 2—The Commuter Zone
or Commutershed; and Zone 3—the Peripheral
Zone. The target population for the year 2000
for Zone 1 is 5,700,000, for Zone 2 300,000
and for Zone 3 2,000,000.